"Larry has given those of us who serve in churches another incredible gift. If you have ever wrestled with the question 'Am I supposed to be a pastor or a leader?' this book is for you. Every chapter is biblical, practical, humorous, and thought provoking."

—GENE APPEL, SENIOR PASTOR, EASTSIDE
CHRISTIAN CHURCH, ANAHEIM, CALIFORNIA

"Some writers pull their content from hours and hours of research and their observations of others. Fortunately for us Larry Osborne writes not from an ivory tower but from his firsthand experience as a leader, pastor, and a mentor to many. In *Lead Like a Shepherd* he shows us how to help move people closer to Jesus, which is ultimately the only valid reason for any of us to serve as a church leader."

—DAVID ASHCRAFT, SENIOR
PASTOR, LCBC CHURCH

"Larry has done it again! He is a master at leadership thinking and offers wisdom for leaders of every age and stage of ministry or marketplace influence. This book is clearly the product of decades of thinking on and living out what does and does not work in regard to leading, inspiring, and serving others. I will be giving this to up-and-coming leaders in our church for a long while."

—MARK CLARK, LEAD PASTOR, VILLAGE
CHURCH, VANCOUVER, BC

"I've been waiting for a book like this for years. The problem with many leadership books is they either neglect a pastor's role as a shepherd or overlook a pastor's role as a leader. *Lead Like a Shepherd* addresses both. Birthed out of decades of pastoral ministry, this book is a treasure trove of leadership principles any church leader, no matter the size or situation, can adopt. Every pastor should have this book on his shelf."

—ROBBY GALLATY, SENIOR PASTOR, LONG
HOLLOW BAPTIST CHURCH; AUTHOR,
GROWING UP AND *THE FORGOTTEN JESUS*

"This is Larry at his best: warm, prophetic, pastoral, insightful, profound, and snarky. He has always been one of my favorite pastors/authors/thinkers, and this book shows you why."

—J. D. GREEAR, PASTOR, THE SUMMIT CHURCH,
RALEIGH-DURHAM, NORTH CAROLINA

"In *Lead Like a Shepherd* Larry Osborne makes an important distinction between leading and discipling and the need for both in order to lead well. Whether you're a senior leader of a church, a small group leader, or a leader at work, if you want to understand how to do both well, you'll want to read this book."

—DAVE FERGUSON, LEAD PASTOR, COMMUNITY
CHRISTIAN CHURCH; AUTHOR, *FINDING YOUR
WAY BACK TO GOD* AND *STARTING OVER*

"One of the most uplifting, encouraging, and practical books on spiritual leadership I've ever read! Balancing humility, wisdom, inspiration, and biblical insight, Larry offers practical instruction even as he reminds us to return to the Good Shepherd as our primary role model. This book is a must-read for anyone called to serve in spiritual leadership."

—CHRIS HODGES, SENIOR PASTOR, CHURCH
OF THE HIGHLANDS; AUTHOR, *FRESH
AIR* AND *THE DANIEL DILEMMA*

"An exceptional read. Dr. Osborne skillfully intertwines the key principles necessary for both effective leadership and discipleship—two topics that rarely coexist in literature. This book will challenge you. I personally recommend it for those desiring to be true to the commission of making disciples."

—JOHN K. JENKINS SR., PASTOR, FIRST BAPTIST
CHURCH OF GLENARDEN, MARYLAND

"*Lead Like a Shepherd* is the best leadership book I've read this year. I am taking our whole staff through it and giving it to all our small group leaders. *Why?* Instead of another shallow, tricks-of-the-trade leadership book, Larry has written a call to live, love, and lead like Jesus!"

—RAY JOHNSTON, FOUNDING PASTOR, BAYSIDE
CHURCH AND THRIVE INTERNATIONAL

"Jesus called himself the Good Shepherd. In *Lead Like a Shepherd* Larry Osborne pushes right to the core of spiritual leadership, where leadership and discipleship go hand in hand. The truths tucked in these pages are essential for every spiritual leader to embrace!"

—JOHN LINDELL, LEAD PASTOR,
JAMES RIVER CHURCH

"*Lead Like a Shepherd* is an incredible discipleship tool for anyone seeking to lead as Jesus did. Osborne's look inside the apostle Peter's teaching, as well as Jesus' example, reveals the stark difference in the way the world defines leadership as opposed to how we, as Christ followers, are called to lead. I recommend this book to anyone who calls Jesus 'Lord.'"

—JOBY MARTIN, LEAD PASTOR,
THE CHURCH OF ELEVEN22

"I have experienced firsthand the issues that occur when leaders are not intentional about both making disciples and empowering leaders. I'm thankful for Larry's focus on teaching both and teaching them well. He is a trusted friend to the ministry I serve, and I am grateful for his voice. I hope this book challenges you to upgrade your leadership skills to lead like a shepherd."

—STEVE MURRELL, PRESIDENT, EVERY
NATION CHURCHES AND MINISTRIES

"There's a perpetual debate in our generation about whether pastors are shepherds or something else. Larry has accomplished an amazing feat. He leads a large church while maintaining a shepherd's heart. Don't read this book unless you want to be convicted that the state of your heart and the style of your leadership matters, no matter what size church you lead."

—CAREY NIEUWHOF, FOUNDING
PASTOR, CONNEXUS CHURCH

"This guy is absolutely amazing. He keeps coming out with one incredible book after another. I don't know how he does it. It must have been his upbringing."

—CAROLYN OSBORNE, LARRY'S MOM

"Of all the leadership models one can pursue in the spiritual realm, Osborne makes the solid case for *shepherd* from a historical, biblical, and personal perspective. *Lead Like a Shepherd* is a great primer for aspiring leaders who want to hang out in the green room, as well as a helpful corrective resource for veteran shepherds still seeking God's will."

—ED STETZER, BILLY GRAHAM DISTINGUISHED
CHAIR, WHEATON COLLEGE

"In today's world when we hear the word *leader*, few people picture a shepherd. But that's exactly the image Larry Osborne wants us to see. I hope you'll read this book and be reminded that whether we're in business or in the ministry, there is no better example we can follow than that of a shepherd."

—GREG SURRATT, FOUNDING PASTOR,
SEACOAST CHURCH; PRESIDENT,
ASSOCIATION OF RELATED CHURCHES

"Larry Osborne is one of the few true spiritual sages I know. Few people can bring practical sense to transcendent topics as he does. I encourage readers to dive into *Lead Like a Shepherd*."

—BRIAN TOME, CROSSROADS CHURCH

LEAD
LIKE A
SHEPHERD

LEAD

LIKE A SHEPHERD

THE SECRET TO LEADING WELL

Larry Osborne

THOMAS NELSON
Since 1798

Published in Nashville, Tennessee, by Thomas Nelson. Thomas Nelson is a registered trademark of HarperCollins Christian Publishing, Inc.

Thomas Nelson titles may be purchased in bulk for educational, business, fund-raising, or sales promotional use. For information, please e-mail SpecialMarkets@ThomasNelson.com.

Any Internet addresses, phone numbers, or company or product information printed in this book are offered as a resource and are not intended in any way to be or to imply an endorsement by Thomas Nelson, nor does Thomas Nelson vouch for the existence, content, or services of these sites, phone numbers, companies, or products beyond the life of this book.

All Scripture quotations are taken from the Holy Bible, New International Version˚, NIV˚. Copyright © 1973, 1978, 1984, 2011 by Biblica, Inc.˚ Used by permission of Zondervan. All rights reserved worldwide. www.zondervan.com. The "NIV" and "New International Version" are trademarks registered in the United States Patent and Trademark Office by Biblica, Inc.˚

ISBN: 978–0718–0964–1–0 (TP)
ISBN: 978–0718–0964–2–7 (e-book)

Library of Congress Control Number: 2017958290

Printed in the United States of America

HB 01.18.2024

To Nancy, Nathan and Marie, Chris and Rachel,
Josh and Kara, William, Emma, Katie, Timothy,
Jonathan, and Jonah. You are the flock that has blessed
me the most. I pray I've loved and led you well.

About Leadership ✳ Network

Leadership Network fosters innovation movements that activate the church to greater impact. We help shape the conversations and practices of pacesetter churches in North America and around the world. The Leadership Network mind-set identifies church leaders with forward-thinking ideas—and helps them to catalyze those ideas resulting in movements that shape the church.

Together with HarperCollins Christian Publishing, the biggest name in Christian books, the NEXT imprint of Leadership Network moves ideas to implementation for leaders to take their ideas to form, substance, and reality. Placed in the hands of other church leaders, that reality begins spreading from one leader to the next . . . and to the next . . . and to the next, where that idea begins to flourish into a full-grown movement that creates a real, tangible impact in the world around it.

NEXT: A Leadership Network Resource
committed to helping you grow your next idea.

LEADERSHIP NETWORK

leadnet.org/NEXT

CONTENTS

CONTENTS

SECTION 4: LEAD BY EXAMPLE

SECTION 5: TAKE THE LONG VIEW

SECTION 1
SPIRITUAL LEADERSHIP

CHAPTER 1

LEAD LIKE A SHEPHERD

I write about leadership and discipleship.

My publishers think it creates "brand confusion." And they compare me to an author who writes cookbooks and mystery novels. They worry that some readers will find it a bit confusing. Am I a Bible teacher or a leadership guy?

But I have my reasons. I believe leadership without discipleship is a waste of time. And discipleship without leadership is an idealistic pipe dream, a recipe for frustration and cynicism.

I find that those who focus solely on leadership tend to take discipleship for granted. They confuse organizational health with spiritual health. They assume that well-run, adequately financed ministries automatically produce disciples. Bigger tends to become synonymous with better, and increased levels of participation are mistaken for increased levels of discipleship.

Now there's obviously nothing wrong with a well-organized, efficient, and growing church or ministry. It sure beats the alternative. But at the end of the day, Jesus didn't call us to create great churches or impressive organizations. He called us to make disciples.[1]

However, a laser-like focus on making disciples is not much better if it downplays or ignores the importance of quality leadership, structures, and systems. These things matter. They're never neutral. They are either working for us or against us. And in the case of those who ignore them, they almost always end up working against them.

I've also noticed that those who focus exclusively on discipleship, evangelism, and the inner life are often cynical toward the local church. They have little patience with those who lag behind because they assume these things are simply a matter of proper commitment and priorities. They don't realize the drag dysfunctional systems and unequipped leadership can have upon the work of the kingdom.

THE TWO SIDES OF THE COIN

The fact is, both leadership and discipleship matter. They are two sides of the same coin.

When a church or ministry is saddled with dysfunctional leaders, outdated traditions, bad systems, or a flawed decision-making process, it will have a hard time making disciples. Church politics and infighting will suck up all the energy and focus that should be on the Great Commission.

But there is also no guarantee that a well-run church will make disciples. Organizational health and spiritual health are two different things. Numerical growth and spiritual growth are not necessarily connected.

And that's the reason for this book. It's a look at the kind of leaders and leadership values that will actually produce disciples rather than merely bigger and better-run churches.

It's not so much about the *task* of leadership as it is about the *heart* of leadership and what it means to lead like a shepherd instead of a CEO.

TESTED BY FIRE

Tragically, I've known more than a few pastors and leaders who spent their lives focused on the size of their flocks rather than the health of their flocks, the task of leadership instead of the heart of leadership. Many had successful ministries. And with their success came the praise of others and the envy of their peers. But I'm pretty sure Jesus wasn't all that impressed.

The apostle Paul warns that if we're not careful, we can build a ministry house that is nothing more than wood, hay, and straw—impressive to look at but incapable of withstanding the fire of God's judgment. And if we do, we'll one day stand before God and experience something akin to losing everything but our lives in a devastating fire.[2]

But it doesn't have to be that way. The Scriptures also promise a totally different outcome for those of us who focus on the heart of leadership and the health of our flocks. Rather than losing everything we've worked so hard to build, we'll find that the flames can't harm it. And better yet, we'll one day receive a "crown of glory that will never fade away" (1 Peter 5:4).

AN ANTIDOTE FOR ARROGANCE

My personal quest to discover what it takes to lead well began after a couple of up-close-and-personal experiences with some of my early ministry heroes.

To my shock and dismay, they proved to be arrogant jerks. The wisdom and warmth they exuded onstage was nowhere to be found in the greenroom or offstage. They were loved by the masses and loathed by those who rubbed shoulders with them daily.

I can't think of anything worse than a lifetime of ministry praised by strangers but despised by those who know me best. So I started searching for mentors and models who could show me a better way. Happily, I found many who followed a different path, pastors and leaders who were more concerned with the health of their flock than the fame of their names.

Around that time I also noticed and began to dial in on the apostle Peter's powerful and simple advice to his fellow ministry leaders: lead like a shepherd.[3]

It struck me as the perfect antidote for the arrogance I'd seen and a practical template that could fit almost any size or type of ministry. Now, decades later, I'm more convinced than ever that his simple paradigm is the missing ingredient in much of our current leadership curriculum.

As we'll discover in the coming pages, a shepherd has a unique leadership style. He doesn't drive his sheep like a cowboy. He doesn't seek to establish himself as an alpha dog, like a trainer, or treat his people as assets to be managed and maximized like a CEO of a publicly traded company.

That's not to say a shepherd doesn't provide strong leadership. He does. A shepherd doesn't ask the sheep where they *want* to go; he leads them fearlessly, confidently, and boldly to where they *need* to go, especially when the sheep don't like it. But we'll save that for later.

THIS BOOK IS FOR YOU

If you are a spiritual leader or aspire to become one, this book is for you.

Don't assume that Peter's leadership advice only applies to those who serve at the top of the leadership food chain. They aren't just for vocational pastors and staff members. They are for *everyone* who provides spiritual leadership. It doesn't matter if the group you lead is large or small, young or old, filled with longtime Christians or folks who are just getting started.

We forget that the early church met primarily in homes, and small homes at that. There were very few large churches and none by today's standards. Extremely limited mobility meant that most were simply neighborhood gatherings of believers.

That means that almost every biblical passage addressed to New Testament leaders (elders, overseers, pastors, deacons, and the like) was written to folks who were leading the equivalent of a modern-day overgrown small group.

Their flocks were not much larger than a Sunday school class. The formal training, theological acumen, and meticulous vetting that we tend to read into these passages simply didn't exist. First-century house churches didn't have seminary-trained pastors, governing boards, or paid staff members. They were led by shopkeepers, tradesmen, and farmers—regular folks who saw it as a privilege to shepherd a small portion of God's great flock.

So it doesn't matter if you're currently a small group leader, a Sunday school teacher, a church planter, a missionary, a denominational executive, or a megachurch pastor; the key to leading others well spiritually is still the same: lead like a shepherd.

All those who do so will one day hear those beautiful words, "Well done, good and faithful servant" (Matt. 25:23).

CHAPTER 2

AM I QUALIFIED?

If you've ever wondered if you're qualified for spiritual leadership, I have some good news.

You probably are.

While not everyone is eligible (the Bible lists some definite disqualifiers), a biblical catalog of the kind of people God chooses to appoint and use as spiritual leaders is filled with folks none of us would have picked. Jesus has a long history of drawing straight lines with crooked sticks.

Who knows? You might be next.

A MAN NAMED PETER

Consider the apostle Peter, the author of the text that we'll be digging into. He suffered the kind of leadership failure most of us would consider fatal to any future ministry plans. He betrayed Jesus. Three times. Even worse, he did so right after brazenly vowing that he would remain loyal to the death.

To his credit, Peter quickly repented. Instead of running away in shame, he faced his failure. Obviously confused and dazed by his disgraceful denials and the horrific death of the one he thought would soon be king, he nevertheless made his way back to the other apostles and huddled up with them as they tried to figure out what to do next.

Then word came that Jesus had burst forth from the tomb. Everything changed.

Well, almost everything. For Peter, the dark cloud of his cowardly denials still loomed large. The once brash, cocky, loudmouthed disciple who'd been the first among equals had been put to the test and failed miserably. I doubt he had any visions of being placed back into leadership. He was just happy to be hanging around the fringes.

But Jesus had other plans.

One morning after breakfast he pulled Peter aside and gave him a new assignment. Sadly, our English translations fail to do justice to the nuances of the conversation. So let's take a closer look.[1]

Jesus started by asking him a question. "Do you love me?"

The word he used for love was *agape*, a Greek word commonly used to describe the highest and most committed type of love—the kind of sacrificial love described in 1 Corinthians 13.

Peter answered, "You know that I love you."

But he used a different Greek word for love. He used *philia*, a word that denoted affection and brotherly love. After his spineless denials, he knew there was no way he could honestly claim to have an *agape* level of love for Jesus.

Yet despite this, Jesus told him, "Feed my lambs."

Then Jesus asked a second time: "Do you love [*agape*]

me?" Peter answered the same way, "You know that I love [*philia*] you." And Jesus reiterated his new assignment, "Take care of my sheep."

But it didn't stop there. Jesus asked a third time. But this time he did something remarkable. He lowered the bar. He used the lesser word for love, *philia*. "Do you love [*philia*] me?"

Distressed and mortified by his failure and, according to the passage, hurt by the fact Jesus asked him a third time, Peter answered, "You know that I *philia* you."

Then Jesus once again reiterated his new assignment: "Feed my sheep."

Think about that for a moment. The arrogant disciple who had fallen the hardest and betrayed Jesus the most was not only reinstated to leadership but rather quickly reinstated at that.

That doesn't mean Jesus ignored or covered up Peter's failings. In fact, he did the opposite. He highlighted them with three pointed questions that were obviously designed to parallel Peter's three denials, and he included the story of the denials in all four Gospels.

It's as if he wanted to make sure Peter (and all of us) would never forget how badly Peter had messed up—or how quickly Jesus put him back to work.

If God only wanted perfect leaders with stellar résumés, he would have left a lot of stories out of the Bible. Peter's is just one example. The privilege of spiritual leadership has never been reserved for those with a perfect track record. It's been reserved for those who repent and run to the cross, no matter who they are or what they've done.

That's why if you're a spiritual leader (or have a desire

to become one) there's no need to hide from your past. And there's no need to pretend in your present. God loves to save and then use the kind of people we'd least expect, people like you, me, and a guy named Peter who, despite his colossal failure—and his inability to look Jesus in the eye and honestly proclaim that he had an *agape*-level of love for him—still had a significant role to play.

RAISING THE BAR

Sadly, we have a long tradition of subtly raising the bar that Jesus came to lower in order to keep out the less than perfect.

It's not a trait unique to Christian leaders. It's a pattern found among all kinds of leaders and professions. For example, my wife is an accountant. There's one thing we've noticed over the years: the many state boards of accountancy are not in the habit of making it easier for applicants to become CPAs. And the same thing happens with doctors, lawyers, professors, arborists, tradesmen, and hairstylists. They all keep finding new ways to raise the bar of entry. It's human nature. Once we're in, we want to keep others out, especially those who are as unqualified to lead as we were when we first started out.

It was a huge problem in the days of Jesus. By the time he showed up, the Jewish standards for spiritual leadership were out of reach for all but the elite.

To serve as a priest you had to have the right pedigree. To become a scribe or scholar you had to be smarter than everyone else. To become a Pharisee you had to jump through an array of extremely difficult hurdles to prove that your self-discipline and intellect were far beyond the norm.

That's one reason why Jesus' choice of his apostles was so confusing to the religious leaders of his day. He broke protocol. Rather than raising the bar, he lowered it. His apostles were a motley crew. That's why the Pharisees, scholars, and other religious leaders had such a disdain for them. In their eyes, they didn't measure up.[2]

Ironically, for the last two thousand years, those of us who call ourselves Jesus followers have tended to pick up right where the Pharisees and scribes left off. We keep making it harder and harder for people to step into leadership roles. We insist upon academic degrees, a deep and nuanced understanding of esoteric theology, experience, an unblemished past, and Navy SEAL-like discipline. It's our way of ensuring we keep out the riffraff, especially the people who are a lot like we used to be.

RÉSUMÉS AND JOB DESCRIPTIONS

Because I pastor a large and highly visible church, I'm often asked by search firms, pulpit committees, and pastors if I know of anyone who might be a good fit for a position they're trying to fill. They often mention they're looking for the caliber of people who serve on our staff.

I usually ask for a job description and a list of the minimum requirements for the job. After I get it, I almost always end up sending a note or email that starts out something like this:

Dear _____:

I'm so pleased that you consider our ministry staff to be filled with the kind of people that you are looking for in order to fill your recently opened staff position. But I regret to inform you that many, if not most, of our current staff members do not meet your minimum requirements for the job—and those that do did not meet them when we first hired them.

Inevitably, the first two qualifications they list as non-negotiables are education and experience. I've yet to see character, anointing, and giftedness at the top of any list.

Now don't get me wrong. I'm not suggesting there shouldn't be some minimum qualifications, but they need to be the right ones. Education and experience aren't determiners of success. They may eliminate some risks. But they don't guarantee godliness or success.

It reminds me of some church planting organizations I work with. A few have fallen into the trap of over assessing. They've raised the bar so high that only the safe and guaranteed-to-be successful can climb over it. Admittedly, they end up with risk-free candidates. And they don't have many failures. But they don't plant many churches either.

They forget that the apostle Paul, the greatest church planter of all time, took huge risks. He wasn't afraid to take a chance. As a result, he planted some pretty lame churches.

That's why he had to write all those letters.

By the way, none of this is meant to imply that we should ignore assessment, overlook sin, or toss out the biblical qualifications for leadership that Paul penned in his letters to

Timothy and Titus. They are important and must be adhered to. Those who ignore them in a mistaken desire to be loving or give a second chance will rue the day.[3]

I am suggesting that when it comes to deciding who's allowed to step into spiritual leadership, the quest for completely risk-free choices is not the way to go. Risk aversion too easily becomes success aversion.

The race doesn't always go to the swift.

Anointing doesn't always fall on the obvious.

The gospel's message of unmerited grace still applies.

It's not just a theological construct to pontificate and debate about; it's a reality we're supposed to live and lead by.

YOU DON'T HAVE TO BE A PROFESSIONAL

I've also noticed that when we think of spiritual leadership, we often assume the apex of serving God is found in what we call full-time or vocational ministry.

That's a tragic mistake.

I wish we'd place a moratorium on two phrases: "called into ministry" and "full-time ministry." Both are theologically incorrect and foster an unbiblical view of professional ministry as somehow being a higher calling than frontline ministry in the marketplace.

We'll talk about that later, but for now, I want to be crystal clear: you don't have to be a professional to be a significant leader in the kingdom of God.

When Jesus cried out, "It is finished!" the temple curtain that separated the Holy of Holies from all but the high priest (who could only enter the Holy of Holies one day a year) was torn from the top down by the finger of God. It was an astounding and unexpected turn of events.

Today, we've become so used to the idea of having direct access to God that this is practically white noise. But for the early Jewish believers it was mind-boggling. The doctrine that we now call the priesthood of believers leveled the playing field in ways they never imagined.[4]

Instead of needing to seek out a Levite priest to make sacrifices that would only temporarily cover their sins, they now had direct access to God through Jesus' once-and-for-all sacrifice.

And whereas spiritual leadership had previously been restricted to those who could meet the strict qualifications of a priest, rabbi, Pharisee, or scribe, it was now open to anyone who could meet the simple qualifications of a shepherd.[5]

RESTORATION

There is still one group for whom spiritual leadership is too often considered out of reach. It's made up of those who were once in leadership but stumbled and fell.

When I reflect upon Peter's restoration, what amazes me most is not that Jesus gave him a second chance after his massive failure. It's the *speed* with which he was reinstated. I'm not always sure what to do with that.

Frankly, I've always been hesitant to put fallen leaders back in the saddle too quickly. I want to make sure they've experienced godly sorrow that leads to repentance, not simply the sorrow that comes from getting caught.[6] And the larger the platform, the more I want to see some significant water flow under the bridge before reinstating them back into a leadership position.

I understand that some people are unfit to lead and some sins are more grievous than others. But I've long had a haunting feeling that perhaps the majority of our formal restoration processes for both lay leaders and clergy may be more onerous and lengthy than Jesus requires. I wonder if we've slowly raised the bar higher than the Scriptures mandate?[7]

Peter

I'm not sure Peter could make the cut in many of our churches today, especially after he blew it again years later by folding under pressure and going along with the legalistic hypocrisy of the so-called Judaizers. Yet he obviously made the cut in God's eyes.[8]

David

I'm almost certain David wouldn't make the cut. In most of our churches, someone with his rap sheet wouldn't be allowed to serve as a pastor or even lead a Sunday school class. Yet God felt he was qualified to pen large chunks of Scripture *after* he'd committed adultery and murder.

That creates an interesting conundrum. Would David ever be allowed to join a pastoral staff and preach in any of our churches? Or would the blogosphere and Twitter world go ballistic? Would we tell him he's unqualified to preach, assign him a seat in the back of the room, and then get up and proclaim to him and everyone else the meaning and application of Psalm 51?

I have to admit, the thought strikes me as odd.

John Mark

When he was a young man, John Mark, the author of the gospel of Mark, went on a mission trip with Paul and Barnabas and bailed out and abandoned them when things got tough. It was a big deal. There was no excuse. It could have cost Paul and Barnabas their lives.

Paul considered John Mark's actions so egregious that he refused to even consider taking him on another trip. But Barnabas wanted to give him another chance. The disagreement between the two over John Mark was so severe that it led to an acrimonious split. Paul and Barnabas went their separate ways and never ministered together again.[9]

Candidly, my natural inclination would be to side with Paul, especially since not much time had passed since John Mark had left them in a lurch. "Abandon me once, shame on you. Abandon me twice, shame on me."

But God seems to have sided with Barnabas. He didn't think John Mark was finished with ministry. He assigned him to write one of the Gospels.

I don't know about you, but I figure if God considers someone qualified to write part of the Bible, he's probably qualified to go on my short-term mission trip.

Just saying.

We talk a lot about grace and mercy.

We claim they're both completely unmerited and impossible to earn.

But when it comes to those who have stumbled and fallen, we tend to change our tune.

The grace and mercy that leads to restoration can easily become something we expect the fallen to earn. *Repentance* becomes a code word for earning their way back into the fold and restoration over a demanding path filled with hurdles we've designed to make sure they're worthy of the grace and mercy they seek. And in some cases, we've actually made our standards for ministry and leadership more restrictive than God's standards for writing Scripture.

Somehow that seems to miss the point. It makes me wonder if we really believe that forgiven means forgiven?

So are *you* qualified to lead?

Unless you're living in high-handed sin, you probably are. You may have some work to do first. But that's what this book is all about.

And if you're a leader already, don't forget that the straight line God has been drawing with your life and ministry is more reflective of the artist's skill than the straightness of the stick.

CHAPTER 3

NO ONE SAID IT WOULD BE EASY

Let's be honest. Spiritual leadership isn't easy.

It's hard work.

Always has been. Always will be.

And sometimes it's more difficult than it is at other times.

We live in one of those times.

It wasn't that long ago that pastors, missionaries, and evangelists were looked up to as role models. They were seen as pillars of the community. Business and government leaders often sought their opinion and approval. Any list of the most admired and trusted professions regularly ranked them near the top.

No longer.

Today, fewer than half of all Americans have a positive view of the ethics and honesty of clergy members.[1] The good news is that we're still way ahead of Congress, journalists, and mass murderers. But it's hard to imagine that's what the apostle Paul had in mind when he insisted that church leaders

21

must be blameless, above reproach, and have a good reputation with outsiders.[2]

I've personally experienced this change in the cultural perception firsthand. I fly a lot. Years ago when a seatmate found out that I was a pastor, he or she would quickly search for a connection point (most often a distant cousin or uncle who served in the ministry somewhere).

Today, the most common response seems to be, *How did I get stuck next to this guy?*

They don't say it out loud. They don't have to. I can see it in their eyes and hear it in their fumbling search for an appropriate response. Sometimes they just open their laptop and put on their headphones to make it clear the conversation is over.

I get it. I do the same thing whenever I'm seated next to someone with a propeller beanie, halitosis, body odor, or a wonderful opportunity in multilevel marketing.

WHO'S TO BLAME?

We certainly bear part of the blame.

Far too many high-profile spiritual leaders have behaved in ways that have brought discredit to the name of Jesus. Many have been less than winsome. Plenty of off-the-radar leaders have messed up as well.

But frankly, that's not the main reason Christian leaders are held in such low regard today. Spiritual leaders behaving badly is nothing new. That has a long history dating back to the earliest days of Scripture. As we've seen, God draws straight lines with crooked sticks.

What is radically different today is that it's no longer our failure to live up to the standards we proclaim that offends people. A large swath of our culture couldn't care less if Christian leaders are immoral or hypocritical. What they're offended by are the standards themselves. Our biblical values have become scandalous.

Within a relatively short time, Jesus and the Bible have gone from being widely honored (if only marginally followed), to grudgingly tolerated, to politically incorrect, to widely vilified as a repressive and dangerous threat.

No one is immune.

Not even Mother Teresa.

EVANGELISM

When the Roman Catholic Church announced that Mother Teresa would be canonized, no one was surprised. Like most people, I expected it. What I didn't foresee was the harsh criticism she received in some circles.

It wasn't from Protestants criticizing her theology. It was from a segment of the cultural elite who criticized her good deeds.

To their way of thinking, her good deeds were anything but good. They were a deceptive guise used to conceal her desire to proselytize and spread allegedly oppressive and dogmatic religious views. And the fact that her ministry focused on serving orphans and the poorest of the poor wasn't a noble thing; it was disgraceful thing, made all the worse because their vulnerability made them easy prey for her evangelistic efforts.

What struck me as culturally significant about their contempt was not its disdain or venom. There will always be critics no matter how much good we do. That's nothing new.

What made it so significant was the way the mainstream media treated it. They reported it as a legitimate contribution to a reasoned and scholarly critique of her work and legacy. They didn't write them off as kooks. They embraced them as thoughtful scholars and pundits.[3]

Think about that for a moment. The idea that evangelism is no longer an acceptable goal for a pastor, evangelist, missionary, or even a Christian has gained enough traction that it's now considered a topic worthy of debate. A culture that once begrudgingly honored Dwight L. Moody, Billy Sunday, and Billy Graham is now open to the notion that good works combined with evangelism is a despicable, deceptive, and subversive behavior.

No wonder my seatmates are so quick to put on their headphones.

FREE SPEECH AND RELIGIOUS FREEDOM

Another cultural shift that makes spiritual leadership more difficult today is our narrowing definition of free speech and religious freedom. They've each lost a lot of traction.

Free speech and religious freedom have always had their limits, and appropriately so. No one argues that we have the right to yell, "Fire!" in a crowded theater when there's no fire or to offer human sacrifices to Baal.

But what has changed is the growing belief within academic, political, and some legal circles that the rights of so-called protected classes take precedence over the rights to free speech and religious freedom. That becomes a significant problem when our ever-broadening definition of protected classes begins to include those who do and celebrate the things the Bible calls sin.

It's one thing to live in a world where sin is legal, common, and widely accepted. The early church did very well in that environment. Frankly, I've never had any desire to force non-Christians to live like Christians. And I've never had much angst over the legalization of sinful behavior. I've always tried to take my cues from the early church. They didn't seem too worried about the decadence and immorality that was legal and prevalent under Roman law. They were much more concerned about the decadence and immorality that was accepted and prevalent within the church.[4]

But it's another thing when merely teaching biblical values within the confines of a sermon or Bible study can be labeled "hate speech" or upholding biblical standards in a faith-based ministry or church is considered not just politically taboo but criminal.

To be clear, I'm not implying the cultural hostility we face today is anything compared to the harsh persecution that many Jesus followers have faced for two thousand years and many still face today. In comparison, we have it easy.

But make no mistake, the die is cast. The question is not *if* the growing cultural hostility toward biblical values will continue but *how quickly* it will move along.

Election cycles and judicial appointments speed up or slow down the process, but the lessons of history are irrefutable.

Once the bastions of higher education, the arts, and the media come into alignment regarding a cultural value or norm, it's only a matter of time until the rest of the culture falls into line.

Unfortunately, all three are already firmly aligned on a number of viewpoints and values that are diametrically opposed to what the Bible teaches. That's going to make it increasingly difficult for a biblically aligned spiritual leader to teach and lead without sounding like a bigot or a cultural Luddite.

BIBLICAL LITERACY

Still another challenge for today's spiritual leaders is a massive decrease in biblical literacy.

Gone are the days when most non-Christians had a vague understanding of the biblical narrative. References to biblical themes and symbols that used to be a standard part of our educational process and vocabulary are now completely missing from the curriculum.

Evangelism is no longer a matter of convincing people that the Jesus story is true. It's now a matter of introducing them to a story they've never heard before.

The same goes for discipling new Christians. We no longer have the advantage of building upon an existing foundation of basic biblical knowledge or even a vague familiarity with it. In many cases, we have to blast before we build, getting rid of a ton of goofy ideas about Jesus and the Bible that have no basis in Scripture.

Even many long-term Christians are woefully ignorant of the Bible. They have a cut-and-paste theology made up of what they think it says, not what it actually says. And good luck to anyone who tries to tell them differently. I've had people tell me their favorite Bible verse and then get angry with me when I point out that such a verse is not actually in the Bible or that the Bible says nothing of the sort.

It reminds me of the WWJD bracelets that were so popular decades ago. People wore them as a reminder to pause and ask "What would Jesus do?"

It was a great idea.

Except for one thing.

Most of the people who wore them had no idea what Jesus said or did.

Modern-day biblical illiteracy is hardly an insurmountable obstacle. Not even close. The early church had to deal with the same problem every time a Gentile came to Jesus.

But it's important to point out that things have changed in our own context. The new norm is ground zero. Those who don't realize it and adjust to it will end up just talking to themselves. It doesn't matter if we're teaching and leading in a local church, a campus ministry, a small group, or even a Bible school. We no longer have the luxury of a head start.

SPIRITUALITY

A final challenge that makes spiritual leadership increasingly difficult today is the hyper privatization of spirituality. It's widely believed that spirituality and our relationship with God is a purely private matter between us and God. All paths lead to the same place as long as we're sincere.

This results in a plethora of spiritual free agents, many of whom are Christians. They march to the beat of their own drummer, which happens to be a mash-up of ideas about Jesus and the Bible. They assume as long as they do what is right in their own eyes, God will be good with it and everyone else should be too.

Unfortunately, when *my* truth becomes more important than *the* truth, the Bible loses its objective authority.

That's why so few people feel the need to dig deeply into Scripture or pursue a biblically aligned life. There's no need to do so when "I've got peace about it" or "I don't think a loving God would do that" carries more weight than a Bible verse.[5]

Free agents also don't sense much of a need for spiritual mentors or leaders. If the final arbitrator of truth is what *I feel* or what *I experienced*, why bother? Most free-agent Christians aren't looking to be discipled; they're looking to be affirmed and encouraged. They'd rather have a cheerleader than a coach.

For example, consider the way tolerance has been redefined in an age of privatized spirituality and customized discipleship. Tolerance used to mean "You have the right to be wrong." But now it means "Everybody is right; so leave me alone."

That has a rather large impact on the way our people respond to biblical leadership. What was once called a loving rebuke or church discipline is now likely to be labeled as meddling or even spiritual abuse.

Clearly, we're not in Kansas anymore. Spiritual leadership is not what it used to be. But don't worry. No one said it would be easy. And God has a plan.

CHAPTER 4

THE ORIGINAL PETER PRINCIPLES

While the headwinds may be strong and the darkness seems to be getting darker, there is no reason for panic or despair.

What we need is a little perspective.

Imagine sitting down with the apostles and complaining about the terrible challenges we face as modern-day Christian leaders in the Western world. I'm not so sure they'd understand our anguish over political marginalization, cultural ridicule, godless court decisions, lost tax deductions, NIMBY[1] lawsuits, and a host of other things we lose sleep over.

The apostles were beaten, chased out of towns, and imprisoned for simply sharing the gospel. All but one died a martyr's death. And the jails they were thrown into were Roman jails, which had no ACLU lawyers to make sure the inmates had decent food, an exercise yard, and plenty of reading material.

I don't think we'd get much sympathy.

LIVING AND LEADING IN TOUGH TIMES

When Peter penned the leadership paradigm that the rest of this book is based upon, he was actually finishing up a larger letter to a group of suffering and confused Christians.

They were mostly Jewish believers who had been driven out of Jerusalem by a great persecution. They were essentially refugees, exiles scattered abroad, fleeing religious oppression. Things weren't going according to plan. It wasn't what they expected as followers of the long-promised Messiah.

Peter wrote to encourage, instruct, and remind them that the things they were going through were nothing new for God's people. Some of their trials and hardships were necessary in order to confirm the genuineness of their faith. Others provided an opportunity to glorify God and show the sharp contrast between righteousness and the decadence of the society they lived in.

And most important, he reminded them that despite all they were going through, after they had suffered for a little while, God himself would restore them, making them strong, firm, and steadfast, fulfilling all of his promises for eternal glory.

Here are just a few passages from his letter to show you what I mean:

> In all this you greatly rejoice, though now for a little while you may have had to suffer grief in all kinds of trials. These have come so that the proven genuineness of your faith—of greater worth than gold, which perishes even though refined by fire—may result in praise, glory and honor when Jesus Christ is revealed. (1 Peter 1:6–7)

Live such good lives among the pagans that, though they accuse you of doing wrong, they may see your good deeds and glorify God on the day he visits us. (1 Peter 2:12)

For it is commendable if someone bears up under the pain of unjust suffering because they are conscious of God. But how is it to your credit if you receive a beating for doing wrong and endure it? But if you suffer for doing good and you endure it, this is commendable before God. To this you were called, because Christ suffered for you, leaving you an example, that you should follow in his steps. (1 Peter 2:19–21)

For you have spent enough time in the past doing what pagans choose to do—living in debauchery, lust, drunkenness, orgies, carousing and detestable idolatry. They are surprised that you do not join them in their reckless, wild living, and they heap abuse on you. (1 Peter 4:3–4)

Dear friends, do not be surprised at the fiery ordeal that has come on you to test you, as though something strange were happening to you. (1 Peter 4:12)

Be alert and of sober mind. Your enemy the devil prowls around like a roaring lion looking for someone to devour. Resist him, standing firm in the faith, because you know that the family of believers throughout the world is undergoing the same kind of sufferings.

And the God of all grace, who called you to his eternal glory in Christ, after you have suffered a little while, will himself restore you and make you strong, firm and steadfast. (1 Peter 5:8–10)

Whew!

Maybe we don't have it so bad.

I'm pretty sure they would have considered the cultural challenges we complain about a welcome relief. Evangelism wasn't just frowned on; it could get you thrown into jail. Free speech and freedom of religion weren't just under attack; they didn't even exist as idealistic concepts. As for biblical literacy? That, too, was completely absent.

Yet this scattered and downtrodden group of early believers was somehow able to join with others to turn the Roman Empire upside down. They literally changed the world. They didn't just survive, they thrived as Christianity spread like wildfire and Jesus built his church in the face of Satan's fiercest attacks.

LEADERS MATTER

It's in this context that Peter penned his leadership paradigm and the simple set of instructions that go with it. He knew that leaders matter. Eventually, every gathering and organization becomes a reflection of its leadership for good or bad. So he chose to end his letter with some final instructions for the leaders.

Peter knew that the success and expansion of the gospel didn't depend upon the ability to wield political power, gain cultural acceptance, or create great Christian institutions. It depended upon the success and health of the tiny house churches God had scattered throughout the region following the rise of the great persecution of the first century.

He knew that a combination of godly leaders and growing disciples would enable the light of Jesus to shine into the darkest of places.

And guess what?

They pulled it off.

The people he wrote to somehow found a way to make a difference without the advantage of big buildings, full-time pastors and staff, seminaries, graphic departments, worship bands, smoke machines, intelligent lights, or video screens. They did it with simple people led by simple leaders who faithfully followed Peter's simple advice: lead like a shepherd.

THE PETER PRINCIPLES

I like to think of Peter's advice to these early church leaders as the original Peter Principles.

If you mention the Peter Principle today, most people, especially business leaders, immediately think of the insights in a 1969 bestseller titled *The Peter Principle: Why Things Always Go Wrong*,[2] which contained observations and research pointing out that most large organizations promote people until they reach their level of incompetence or unpromotability. Once they arrive there, they stay there until they retire or die. The authors believed this was the reason most bureaucracies and large institutions are generally incompetent: they eventually reach a point where every position is characterized by ineptitude.

They were obviously on to something. Most of us have firsthand experiences validating these observations, which explains why the book still sells well almost half a century later.

But long before Dr. Laurence Peter explained why nothing works like it's supposed to, the apostle Peter penned his own Peter Principles. They were built upon the simple concept that in order to lead well we need to lead like shepherds:

> To the elders among you, I appeal as a fellow elder and a witness of Christ's sufferings who also will share in the glory to be revealed: Be shepherds of God's flock that is under your care, watching over them—not because you must, but because you are willing, as God wants you to be; not pursuing dishonest gain, but eager to serve; not lording it over those entrusted to you, but being examples to the flock. And when the Chief Shepherd appears, you will receive the crown of glory that will never fade away. (1 Peter 5:1–4)

In the following chapters we'll dig deeply into this "lead like a shepherd" leadership paradigm. We'll break Peter's appeal into four simple, profound exhortations that can work for anyone anywhere when they take on the mantle of spiritual leadership. Those four exhortations are:

1. Think like a shepherd.
2. Serve with enthusiasm.

3. Lead by example.
4. Take the long view.

So let's get going. Let's find out what it's like to live out Peter's two-thousand-year-old leadership principles in a twenty-first-century context. I guarantee that you'll find leading like a shepherd to be every bit as powerful today as it was in the first century. Maybe even more so.

SECTION 2
THINK LIKE A SHEPHERD

To the elders among you, I appeal as a fellow elder and a witness of Christ's sufferings who also will share in the glory to be revealed: Be shepherds of God's flock that is under your care.

—1 PETER 5:1–2

CHAPTER 5

IT'S ALL ABOUT THE SHEEP

First-century shepherds were hardly the romanticized figures found in today's children's classes and nativity scenes. They were social outcasts at the bottom of the ancient world's food chain. They were a necessary cog in the economy, but they were nothing anyone wanted to aspire to be when they grew up.

Herding sheep was a dirty, boring job with crazy-long hours. In the family hierarchy, the task of shepherding the family herd almost always fell to the youngest and least distinguished son, which explains why Jesse didn't even think of David when the prophet Samuel came to interview and anoint one of Jesse's sons as the next king.[1]

If you had a lot of sheep and no sons, you hired someone to do the job. But good help was hard to come by. Shepherding was a low-paying, low-prestige, transient occupation filled by those on the fringes of society. And hirelings were notoriously undependable. They were known to bail at the first sign of trouble or danger. They were considered so untrustworthy they weren't allowed to testify in a court of law.

So don't be fooled by the fact that so many biblical heroes were once shepherds. That didn't impress the Jews of Jesus' day enough to view shepherding as a noble profession. But it did cause them to marvel at God's propensity to choose and bless the most unlikely of people, including shepherds like Abraham, Jacob, Moses, David, and Amos, to name a few.

A NEW PARADIGM: IT'S ALL ABOUT THE SHEEP

Yet despite the low status of shepherds in ancient culture, the metaphor of leaders as shepherds was common in both pagan and Jewish literature. There are a number of reasons why.

The shepherd metaphor portrayed kings and leaders as the primary source of care, concern, and protection for their subjects. It emphasized the people's utter dependence on their kings, priests, and leaders, since sheep are notoriously incapable of fending or caring for themselves.

In the Old Testament, the shepherd imagery was applied to spiritual leaders, both good and bad. Ezekiel railed on the self-serving priests and leaders of Israel as shameful shepherds worthy of judgment, and he promised that God himself would one day step in to shepherd his own flock.[2] And of course, the famous Psalm 23 paints the Lord as our great shepherd.

But Jesus radically changed the shepherding paradigm. He didn't just call himself the Good Shepherd, he also proclaimed that the mark of a good shepherd is his willingness to sacrifice his life for the sheep.

I am the good shepherd. The good shepherd lays down his life for the sheep. The hired hand is not the shepherd and does not own the sheep. So when he sees the wolf coming, he abandons the sheep and runs away. Then the wolf attacks the flock and scatters it. The man runs away because he is a hired hand and cares nothing for the sheep. (John 10:11–13)

Don't let the familiarity of this passage blind you to its mind-blowing and paradigm-shifting significance. Jesus didn't say that good shepherds care, feed, lead, and protect their sheep. He said they lay down their lives for their sheep.

If those words mean anything, one thing is crystal clear. When it comes to being a New Testament shepherd, it's all about the sheep, not the shepherd.

ASKING THE WRONG QUESTION

As Jesus pointed out, there is a big difference between a shepherd and a hireling. One of the major differences can be seen in the questions they ask. The shepherd asks, "What do the sheep need?" The hired hand asks, "What's in it for me?"

Unfortunately, many of us in spiritual leadership have been taught to ask the hireling question. It's not just our human nature, it's a deeply rooted part of our culture. Anyone who has recently interviewed job applicants knows exactly what I mean. It's not unusual for the applicant to have more demands than the employer.

Even in seminary I was told to make sure that a church

didn't take advantage of me. I was shown how to set firm boundaries, be true to myself, and make sure I wasn't treated like a servant or a slave.

I understand where they were coming from. There are far too many dysfunctional ministries out there that can tear a person or family apart. And there's no need to walk into the lion's den unless God has specifically sent you there.

But didn't Jesus say something about the path to greatness being found on the same path as that of a servant or a slave? And didn't he say that since he laid down his life for us, we're supposed to do the same for others?[3]

It seems that many of us like the idea of servant leadership. We're more than willing to take the back seat, wash dishes, help set up or clean up, even wash dirty feet, as long as everyone knows we're the leader. But when someone actually treats us like a servant, we're quick to take offense.

That's one of the main reasons so many of us bail out of a commitment or leadership position at the first sign of hardship or the realization that we've been taken advantage of (which in most cases means we are giving more than we get in return).

Too often our sin nature, coupled with our "watch out for number one" culture, has made the wrong question seem like the right question. And whenever that happens, it's hard to lead a flock well. It doesn't matter if it's a small Bible study group or an entire congregation.

The right question is always, "What do the sheep need?"

It's what a real shepherd asks.

IT'S A CALLING, NOT A CAREER

I remember when I was first exploring my options to become a senior pastor. The denominational executive I met with suggested I take on a "stepping-stone church." By that he meant a dying church that was already on life support.

He wasn't asking me to go there and revitalize or restart it. It wasn't that kind of church. He wanted me to go there and bide my time until a better opportunity came along. He told me not to worry. It wouldn't be for long. It was the perfect proving ground. As long as I didn't mess up, it would open lots of doors for something better in the future.

I was taken aback by his candor and cynicism.

Something inside me kept whispering that ministry is a calling, not a career. So even though I was young and hardly a desirable candidate, my wife and I said no. We couldn't imagine going anywhere with the intent of using the people and their church as a stepping-stone. It just seemed wrong.

But the denominational executive obviously had no problem with it.

That's because he saw ministry as a career. He assumed my goal was to climb the ministry ladder. And while he wanted me to serve the dying congregation well, he didn't see serving them as an end in itself. It was simply the next step on a path to a better opportunity.

Fortunately, it wasn't long before I found another tribe and a mentor who thought differently. Instead of treating ministry as a career, he affirmed that it was a calling. And while God might call me to serve in different places at different times, the determining factor of when and where should always be God's calling, not what's best for my career.

There are no stepping-stone churches. There is only the bride of Christ. Some churches are in good shape. Some aren't. Some have a great future. Some only have a past. But they all belong to Jesus. And none of them are meant to be stepping-stones.

Staying the Course

Eventually a ministry opportunity opened up in an area where my wife and I felt we could settle in for the long haul, maybe a lifetime. It was a brand-new church plant, a little more than a year old, meeting in a high school cafeteria with the remnants of food fights on the wall. I had to take a big cut in pay to go there, but that was offset by my new office in a parishioner's garage and a secondhand desk I found in the trash at the big church where I'd previously been a youth pastor.

I thought I'd died and gone to heaven.

What more could I ask? God had given us a clear sense of his calling to a specific church and location. The church had agreed. We were certain (at least I was sure) that within a few years we'd have a thriving ministry on our hands.

Unfortunately, that's not what happened.

Things didn't go so well.

We grew. But it was by only one person during the first three years.

To make matters worse, there was nothing to indicate that things would be any different in the near future. If we stayed put, it looked like this would be our lot in life. I'd spend the rest of my life pastoring a church much smaller than any of my old youth groups, and we'd grow by approximately ten people a decade.

It was hardly what I had in mind when I was so certain that God was calling us to northern San Diego.

Finally, things started to slowly turn around. The church experienced some modest growth. After five years, I was able to hire another staff member to help me pastor the church. Then out of nowhere I received a letter. It was from the pulpit committee of a church I had long looked up to as the kind of church I hoped North Coast would be someday. They wanted to know if I wanted to be considered for their senior pastor opening.

Don't ask me why.

I have no idea.

Especially based on my track record and résumé at the time.

But I was pumped. I remember reading the letter and immediately fast-forwarding to all the great things God would do once I had a larger and more prestigious platform. I thought he was giving me a "get out of jail free" card.

But as I basked in the possibilities, I distinctly heard that still, small voice (the one we sometimes wish we could drown out) say, *I called you here, not there.*

I thought, *Rats!*

But the prompting was so strong and clear that I knew not to ask again.

So I tossed the letter.

A few of those closest to me were incredulous, including some family members. They were sure I'd made the wrong decision. They couldn't imagine why God would want me to waste my gifts and potential on what was obviously a dead-end ministry, especially when a much better and larger platform beckoned. They thought it was career suicide.

Obviously, it wasn't. Obedience never is.

To say the least, things have gone rather well since then. But I have often wondered where I would be today if I'd approached ministry and leadership like the denominational executive who wanted me to take a stepping-stone church.

What if I'd asked the hireling's question?

What if I'd bought into the lie that ministry is a career, not a calling?

HOW DO WE KEEP SCORE?

All of us keep score. It's human nature. We can't help it. Even those who claim they don't actually do. We're all like the parents at a T-ball game where scorekeeping is forbidden. Somehow when the last inning comes, everyone knows when their kid hits the game-winning home run or makes the game-losing error.

The problem with scorekeeping is not keeping score. It's having the wrong goal.

My dad taught us a game when we were kids. He called it giveaway checkers. Instead of capturing the other player's pieces, the goal was to be the first one to run out of checkers. The only rule was that you had to jump and capture any vulnerable checker.

It's was a great metaphor for life, marriage, and leadership. If I'm keeping score to make sure the other guy has gotten more than I have, keeping score is a good thing.

Unfortunately, many of us keep score like a hired hand. We want to make sure we're always ahead in the count, getting more than we give.

But the path to success in God's kingdom has always been to give more than we get. Those who lose on their earthly scorecard inevitably win on God's eternal scorecard. And that's the only one that counts.

Jesus put it this way when a much younger and less wise Peter drilled him about the earthly rewards he and his fellow disciples could expect in return for all they had given up to follow Jesus:

> Truly I tell you, at the renewal of all things, when the Son of Man sits on his glorious throne, you who have followed me will also sit on twelve thrones, judging the twelve tribes of Israel. And everyone who has left houses or brothers or sisters or father or mother or wife or children or fields for my sake will receive a hundred times as much and will inherit eternal life. But many who are first will be last, and many who are last will be first. (Matt. 19:28–30)

CALLED OR ENTICED?

Finally, if you're a pastor, have you noticed that few of us are ever called to a smaller church in a less desirable community? It seems that every time God calls one of us to a new ministry, it's bigger, better, or more prestigious than the old one.

And the few times when we feel called to a smaller platform or lower profile ministry, it's almost always on the heels of a miserable or untenable situation that makes trading down seem like a step up.

Now don't get me wrong. I'm not implying that spiritual leaders should seek out the least rewarding, most difficult path and take it. Or that every spiritual leader should stick it out no matter how miserable the experience might be. That's an old-school poverty gospel. That's not the path of discipleship; it's the path of a spiritual masochist.

The apostles didn't stick around to see if their enemies would throw them into jail again. Jesus even told them to shake the dust off their feet and move on if they found themselves unwanted. And Paul sought to go to Rome in an attempt to increase his influence and to have a greater platform from which to proclaim the gospel.[4]

And I'm certainly not advocating that every pastor needs to spend a lifetime in one place or stay around no matter what. Even those of us who feel called to do so need to keep an open mind. If the apostle Paul couldn't accurately figure out ahead of time the details of God's will and game plan, we shouldn't assume we can either.[5]

I'm simply saying that whenever the hireling question becomes my leading question, I won't shepherd well. And whenever ministry becomes a career, it ceases to be a calling.

CHAPTER 6

WILLING TO BE MISUNDERSTOOD

Peter's original audience knew a lot more about shepherding than most of us do. They didn't have to go to the county fair to see sheep. They were plentiful in the nearby hills. And since his readers were mostly Jewish believers, they also would have been familiar with Psalm 23, the most famous passage about shepherding in the Bible.

In the next few chapters we'll take a deep dive into Psalm 23. We'll discover some hidden gems and powerful insights that will be new to many of us but were blindingly obvious to Peter's first-century readers.

The most famous translation of Psalm 23 is in the King James Bible. The eloquence of the old Shakespearian dialect has rendered it into a cultural icon. But it's also caused most of us to miss a few things since we no longer use Shakespearian English outside of drama class. So let's look at it in a more modern translation:

The LORD is my shepherd, I lack nothing.
    He makes me lie down in green pastures,
he leads me beside quiet waters,
    he refreshes my soul.
He guides me along the right paths
    for his name's sake.
Even though I walk
    through the darkest valley,
I will fear no evil,
    for you are with me;
your rod and your staff,
    they comfort me.
You prepare a table before me
    in the presence of my enemies.
You anoint my head with oil;
    my cup overflows.
Surely your goodness and love will follow me
    all the days of my life,
and I will dwell in the house of the LORD
    forever.

Now the first thing to notice about how the Lord shepherds us is that he does what is best for us whether we like it or not. In other words, he's willing to be misunderstood. Let's read it again, this time noticing the phrases I've italicized:

The LORD is my shepherd, I lack nothing.
    He makes me lie down in green pastures,
he leads me beside quiet waters,
    he refreshes my soul.

He guides me along the right paths
   for his name's sake.
Even though I walk
   through the darkest valley,
I will fear no evil,
   for you are with me;
your rod and your staff,
   they comfort me.
You prepare a table before me
   in the presence of my enemies.
You anoint my head with oil;
   my cup overflows.
Surely your goodness and love will follow me
   all the days of my life,
and I will dwell in the house of the LORD
   forever.

HE MAKES ME LIE DOWN

I always assumed that the green pastures and quiet waters were symbols of God's extravagant care. I imagined an idyllic setting. I never noticed the words "makes me."

They are rather important. They imply resistance. No one *makes* their kids do things they *want* to do. We only have to *make* them do the things they *don't* want to do.

It's no news flash that sometimes the Lord has to *make us* lie down in green pastures.

Perhaps you've found yourself stuck in a situation you didn't want to be in. You wondered what God was up to. You may even have reacted with bewilderment, frustration, and anger. But years later, with the 20/20 clarity of hindsight, you looked back and realized that he put us exactly where we needed to be.

That's what making us lie down in green pastures is all about.

Every shepherd has to occasionally make his sheep do something they don't want to do. It's an unpleasant but necessary part of leadership. A good shepherd doesn't take a poll to see where the sheep *want* to go. He finds out where the sheep *need* to go and then leads them there.

As far as I can tell, the only instance in the Bible where the sheep took a vote didn't work out too well. It was the ultimate congregational meeting gone bad. The flock decided that the promised land was too dangerous to move into, so they turned around and headed back into the desert. It was not a good decision. It was a disaster for everyone involved. Except the Canaanites. It worked out pretty well for them. They got an extra thirty-nine years out of it.[1]

THE FRUSTRATIONS OF LEADERSHIP

The longer I lead, the more convinced I am that it's impossible to lead well if we aren't willing to be misunderstood.

I mentor lots of young leaders. One thing I always tell them is that they have to develop thick skin and an ability to live with low-level frustration. They usually think I'm talking about the internal frustrations of leadership.

But I'm not.

I'm referring to the low-level frustrations directed at them, not in them. Our sheep seldom know what's best for them. If they did, they wouldn't need shepherds. When we have to force them to do something they don't want to do (even if it's lying down in a green pasture), they tend to get angry, post crazy stuff on social media, and complain about it to all their friends.

It's what frustrated sheep do.

If you want to be a shepherd, you'd better get used to it.

SOME THINGS CAN'T BE EXPLAINED

It can be incredibly wearisome to do something for the benefit of others only to have them react as if you're leading them off a cliff. But a good shepherd is willing to take the heat. He realizes there are some things the sheep will never understand.

It reminds me of what a modern-day shepherd has to do when there's an outbreak of lice in the flock. The only way to keep it from spreading is to plunge each lamb, one by one, into a cleansing chemical solution. And when I say plunge, I mean plunge.[2]

Each member of the flock is led up a ramp and into a dip. The dip is about thirty feet long and has to be deep enough for the sheep to be completely submerged. After they're plunged into it, they have to swim in it for at least thirty seconds, and then the shepherd has to dunk their head under the water by pushing it back and down at the same time. And he has to do it twice.

Now think about that for a moment. Sheep build an emotional bond with their shepherd. So much so that they know his voice and follow him wherever he goes. It's a relationship of trust developed over time.

Yet once the flock has been hit with a lice infestation, the shepherd has to take each of his trusting lambs up a ramp and then suddenly, without any explanation, plunge them into the dip. And as soon as each lamb gets its head back above water, the shepherd has to shove it back down again. I guarantee you that his sheep don't understand. They've got to be thinking, *What's up with that?* and a few other things that can't be printed in a Christian book.

But here's the worst part from a shepherd's perspective.

There's no way to explain what just happened. It can't be done. Ever. The sheep will always be in the dark. Shepherds can't speak Sheep or whatever it is that sheep speak.

The same thing holds true in a ministry setting. There are always going to be some things you will have to do but no one will understand. It's one of the most painful parts of leadership, especially for those of us who want everyone to like (or at least agree with) us.

It might be remaining faithful to a biblical precept that everyone wants to ignore.

It might be a ministry vision that no one else sees.

It might be spiritual cancer that needs to be cut out while everyone wants to pretend it's not there.

I can't say what it will be about or where it will happen.

But it will happen.

Guaranteed.

THE SCARY PATH

There's another section of Psalm 23 that speaks to this issue of being misunderstood. But most of us miss it. I know I did for years.

It's found in the third and fourth verses of the psalm: "He guides me along the right paths for his name's sake. Even though I walk through the darkest valley . . ."

Frankly, I never connected being guided along the right path with the valley of darkness. I thought one verse spoke of the Lord showing us the path of righteousness that brings glory to his name, and the other spoke about his presence even in life's darkest moments, especially the one that leads to death.

But that's not what the passage says. The two actually go together, as you can see above. The point the psalmist is making is that the Lord leads us on the right path for his name's sake *and* that path inevitably takes us through dark valleys on the way to the mountaintop.

First-century Christians wouldn't have missed this connection, because they would have known the annual grazing pattern that flocks follow in the rolling hills of the Holy Land as the weather changes.

Every summer the grass at the lower elevations would be grazed over and dry. The only green grass was higher up the mountain. So a shepherd would lead his sheep up the mountain to the places where the grass was still lush and plentiful.

Unfortunately, the only way to get to the higher elevations was to travel through narrow and dangerous valleys. Their ancient paths followed the same routes our highways do today.

To get to the top you have to follow the contours of the valley. It's the only way up unless you're into free climbing and repelling. And rumor has it that sheep don't do either very well.

It's tough enough when we have to *make* our sheep lie down in green pastures. But at least after a bite or two of the lush grass they're likely to realize it's not so bad after all.

It's really tough when we have to lead them through a dangerous and scary valley filled with predators—and all the while have no way to explain to them that it's the only way to survive.

But isn't that exactly what the Lord does in our lives? He takes us where we need to go, not where we want to go. He leads us on the path of righteousness for his name's sake, but it's often a scary and dangerous path that makes us wonder what he's up to or if he still cares about our well-being.

SPIRITUAL BULLIES

There are some shepherds who relish the idea of tough love. They seem to like forcing their sheep to lie down and taking them places they don't want to go. They don't shy away from conflict; they run to it.

If that's the kind of shepherd you tend to be, you've probably loved this chapter—so far.

But I want to be clear. A good shepherd will put the need of the sheep first, even at the risk of being misunderstood and maligned. But he doesn't enjoy it. Those who enjoy keeping their sheep on edge aren't shepherds, they're spiritual bullies.

They remind me of a pastor I once knew.

He was bright, passionate, and a strong communicator.

He was also a bit of an idealist. By his own admission, he didn't like many of the people in his church. He thought they were uncommitted, lazy wimps.

When he took the lead pastor role in a large church that had been in decline for a number of years, he thought he'd have no problem turning things around. At first, it looked like he was right. The crowds swelled, thanks to his strong communication skills. Some good things were done.

But the longer he was there, the more impatient he became. Whenever something needed to be changed (and believe me, there was a boatload of things that needed to be changed), he ignored the softer sides of leadership. He went right into "makes me" and "leads me into the valley" mode.

After a few years it became evident that he had two fatal leadership flaws: (1) he was too impatient to slow down and earn the trust of his flock and (2) he found a perverse joy in shocking and scaring the sheep he thought moved too slowly.

It's no surprise that he didn't last very long.

But it wasn't because he didn't know where the green pastures were or how to make his sheep lie down in them.

It wasn't because he didn't know his way through the valley to the mountaintop.

It was because he had the heart of a hireling.

He didn't know the difference between being misunderstood and maligned and being distrusted and despised. He was a spiritual bully, not a shepherd.

Those who learn to lead with a shepherd's heart won't always be loved and understood. But they'll wish they were. Those who lead with a hireling's heart won't give a rip—at least not until they find themselves in the unemployment line.

CHAPTER 7

ADAPTING TO WEAKNESS

There are two sides to every coin.

In the last chapter we saw the importance of strong and forceful leadership—why we must be willing to *make* our flock do the right thing even when they don't want to do it. But the other side of the shepherding coin is just as important. It's the willingness to patiently adapt and adjust to the fears and weaknesses of the flock, to meet them where they are, not where they ought to be.

I'm always surprised at how many pastors and spiritual leaders seem to think that the forceful side of leadership is the only side and that acquiescing to the fears and weaknesses of their people is a form of spiritual compromise.

It's not.

It's actually quite like Jesus.

He gave mercy to a woman caught in the act of adultery—not a woman who came forward to repent of her adultery. He told a parable about a tax collector being justified because he simply asked for mercy—not after he quit his job and cleaned up his act. He healed the son of a man with inadequate faith, and he was a friend of sinners, not just former sinners.[1]

Yes, I know that Jesus told them to go and sin no more. But he didn't wait for them to measure up before offering compassion and forgiveness. He went and met them in their sin and failure, called them to himself, and then told them, "Go and sin no more."

Once again, David's portrayal of the Lord as our ideal shepherd in Psalm 23 speaks powerfully to the issue at hand. It shows us what it looks like to compassionately adapt and adjust to their fears and limitations.

But, unfortunately, our lack of familiarity with real sheep and real shepherds has caused many (if not most) of us to miss the obvious.

QUIET WATERS

David points out that along with making us lie down in green pastures, the Lord also "leads me beside quiet waters."

As I noted earlier, I used to picture the green pastures and quiet waters as a depiction of God's lavish blessings and favor. I imagined a lush meadow with some trees and a stream running through it, a great place to read a book or take a nap. But that's not what David had in mind. He wasn't talking about the beauty of a lush meadow. He was describing an arduous task that a shepherd had to do daily.

Sheep need water. But they're afraid of moderate-to-fast-moving streams. So a free-range shepherd had to make sure his sheep were always near water that was slow moving or dammed. And whenever there wasn't any nearby, he had to dam it himself. Otherwise the sheep wouldn't drink.

Ironically, running water is purer and healthier. The faster the better. And unless we're talking about genuine rapids, moving water presents no real danger to the sheep. Especially when their shepherd is standing nearby, staff in hand, ready to pluck out any who stumble or appear to be in danger of being washed downstream.

It must have been frustrating for a shepherd to constantly search for still water or have to dam up a portion of the stream when the only reason it was necessary was his flock's stubborn refusal to drink from running water.

I would have been tempted to sit down and wait for them to get thirsty enough to drink anyway, much like I did when my kids refused to eat what Mom put before them. They had two choices: eat it or go to bed hungry. Problem solved.

But that's not what a good shepherd does. He adapts to the weaknesses and limitations of his flock even when those fears and limitations are unfounded and frustrating. He knows his job is to keep them healthy and hydrated, no matter what it takes to get the job done.

ANGRY SHEPHERDS

Unfortunately, I find that many of us in positions of spiritual leadership are far too impatient, idealistic, or lazy to do the kind of adapting and adjusting that a real shepherd like David did daily.

I speak at a lot of conferences. I've noticed that whenever a group of ministry leaders get together (especially professionals like pastors, missionaries, and theology professors), there is a lot of talk and criticism of inwardly focused churches, consumer Christians, rampant spiritual immaturity, and ministries that aren't growing or multiplying fast enough.

But that's all there is. A lot of talk and criticism directed at the sad state of the church and discipleship. Nothing more. Just talk.

These folks are what I call angry shepherds. They don't love their flocks. They don't even like them. They aren't willing to lift a finger to help make it easier for folks to come to Jesus or less demanding to follow him. And they're quick to accuse anyone who does so of selling out, watering down the gospel, or failing to take the cost of discipleship seriously.

I get the strong impression they'd rather thin the herd than care for their sheep. They want a church full of special forces disciples and wish everyone else would stay away.

But angry shepherds, disgusted and dismayed by the shortcomings of their sheep, don't advance the cause of Jesus. They may think they're helping out, but they're not. In reality, they have far more in common with the Pharisees of Jesus' day than the Great Shepherd in David's psalm.

ALL THINGS TO ALL PEOPLE

The apostle Paul provides a great example of what adapting and adjusting looks like. He was quick to modify his message and methods to the weaknesses and blind spots of his audience. He described his approach to ministry this way:

> Though I am free and belong to no one, I have made myself a slave to everyone, to win as many as possible. To the Jews I became like a Jew, to win the Jews. To those under the law I became like one under the law (though I myself am not under the law), so as to win those under the law. To those not having the law I became like one not having the law (though I am not free from God's law but am under Christ's law), so as to win those not having the law. To the weak I became weak, to win the weak. I have become all things to all people so that by all possible means I might save some. I do all this for the sake of the gospel, that I may share in its blessings. (1 Cor. 9:19–23)

No surprise, he was harshly criticized in some circles for making it too easy for people to come to Jesus, especially Gentiles. So don't be dismayed when the same thing happens to you when you make significant adaptations and adjustments to accommodate the weaknesses and limitations of your flock.

Not everyone will appreciate your efforts to provide quiet waters. They didn't appreciate Jesus' efforts or the apostle Paul's. Why should they appreciate yours? The religious elite have always leaned toward making it harder for people to come in, not easier. They tend to see their role as keeping the unworthy out, not inviting them in.

But don't worry. You will be in good company, assuming you consider Jesus, the apostle Paul, and the Father to be good company.

In the next few chapters we'll take a closer look at what it means to adapt and adjust to the weaknesses and limitations of our flocks in a modern-day context. We'll explore some practical, real-life examples of what it means to dam up the water so our sheep will drink.

Don't get hung up by any of the specific examples. They aren't prescriptions. They're descriptions. They illustrate some of the things I've done in my own ministry context to adapt and adjust to the cultural blind spots, fears, and spiritual failings that keep my flock from experiencing God's best.

Some of the things we've done will apply and some won't. But each of them illustrates the kind of issues that every modern-day spiritual leader has to deal with, whether the flock we lead is young or old, tiny or massive.

CHAPTER 8

ADAPTING TO BLIND SPOTS

Blind spots are unavoidable. We all have them. Some are unique to us as individuals and some are fairly common and widespread.

It would be great if we could remove blind spots by simply pointing them out—and if everyone would thank us for doing so. But it doesn't work that way. Blind spots aren't simply areas of ignorance easily corrected with new information. They are literally blind spots. We can't see them, and we don't tend to believe it when someone else tries to point them out to us.

One of the most frustrating things a shepherd has to deal with are what I call "cultural blind spots." They're essentially a form of group think, which is what makes them so hard to overcome. Once everyone believes something, most of us will go along with everyone, no matter what the facts are. And those few outliers who see what we can't see and refuse to go along are written off as curmudgeons or fools.

By the way, blind spots are different from the high-handed

sins that some people want to ignore because everyone else allegedly does it. A good shepherd works around blind spots, but he roots out sin and rebellion. We'll explore that important aspect of shepherding later, but for now, we're dealing with genuine blind spots, the wrongheaded cultural values, beliefs, and priorities that are most common and prevalent in our flocks today.

QUIRKY OR DANGEROUS?

Some cultural blind spots are simply quirky. They cause us to believe things that aren't true and to do things that are foolish. They don't do much harm.

But others are incredibly harmful and dangerous. For instance, no one seemed to notice the perils of smoking or building with asbestos until the damage was done. Magazine ads and press releases actually extolled their health and lifestyle benefits. Most of the people who smoked or handled asbestos had no idea they were dealing with death. And even after the alarms were sounded, people were slow to believe the warnings. It was a huge and tragic blind spot.

In the spiritual realm, the same thing happens. Some of our blind spots are simply quirky. But others are incredibly dangerous. It's the shepherd's job to confront, work around, and protect the flock from the dangerous ones.

A New Definition of Love

For example, most people today think that loving someone means strongly encouraging and affirming them in their choices, no matter what choices they make. It's not our job to judge. It's our job to love.

This has made it extremely difficult for many in our flocks to accept the hard sayings of Jesus, especially those that call for significant and extended self-restraint, deprivation, or self-denial.

Consider the way our definition of biblical sexual purity has changed. And I'm not talking about the same-sex attraction debates. I'm talking about the way most people in our churches look at every area of sexuality. Thanks to our culture's current definition of love—which mostly focuses on making sure nobody has a bad day—anything that calls for extreme or extended self-denial is written off as harsh, legalistic, unrealistic, and cruel.

Many in our flocks have set aside significant portions of the Bible and the Gospels in their pursuit of being more loving and more like Jesus. And they see no irony in it.

They've bought into the original lie of Satan: "Did God really say . . . ?" (Gen. 3:1). And they've decided he's right; there's no way a loving God could have said or expected that. It's too difficult and painful to expect anyone to live that way.

Maximizing Potential

The mad pursuit of maximized potential as the ultimate purpose in life is another modern-day cultural blind spot that most of us will have to deal with.

Maximized potential has become the North Star by which most people—Christians included—make big decisions. It's an unquestioned priority in most of our households. It explains why helicopter parents hover and why church attendance is no longer a top priority in many Christian homes.

Here's how it works and some of the things we've done to adapt and adjust so our flock won't starve to death.

T-Ball and D-1 Scholarships

A five-year-old hits a homerun in T-ball. His parents suddenly realize that he might get a D-1 scholarship. So they immediately enroll him in a program so he can get the right coaching, play against the right players, and maximize his newfound potential to the fullest.

While his parents hate the fact that they frequently miss church because most of the tournaments are on weekends and all the championship games are on Sunday, they don't see any other option. It's when the big games are played. What can they do?

After all, they have to maximize his potential.

It's what good parents do.

Isn't it?

What they don't realize is that no matter how much they maximize their son's athletic prowess and no matter how many doors they open for his future, he has, at best, a tiny chance of making his high-school team. As for getting a scholarship, the odds are near zero. And the odds of playing in the big leagues? They're infinitesimal.

On the other hand, the odds are incredibly high (nearly 100 percent) that he will learn the life lesson that his parents are unintentionally teaching him: church is important . . . unless there is something more important.

Even worse, most of these parents are oblivious to the fact that while our children tend to adopt our values, they seldom adopt our boundaries. If I lie to the IRS or call in sick to spend the day at Disneyland with my kids, I shouldn't be surprised when they lie to me about where they were last night.

In the same way, parents who consistently skip church to maximize their child's athletic prowess shouldn't be surprised when he goes away to college and skips church to sleep in, catch up on homework, or anything else he considers to be important.

Yet try telling that to most parents today.

You won't get far.

They won't listen.

Because they can't. It's a cultural blind spot.

They're blinded by our culture's obsession with potential. They take it as a given that no decent parent would even think of squandering a child's potential. It's not an option.

Now obviously, baseball is not the only culprit. There are club programs and traveling squads for anything a child is gifted at: baseball, basketball, volleyball, hockey, soccer, drama, music, academics, and tiddlywinks.

QUIET WATERS

As a shepherd, I have a choice to make.

I can rail against skewed priorities and the folly of placing athletics, academics, and the performing arts above spiritual development. I can wait for families to get spiritually thirsty enough to skip the next tournament. I can write a series of blog posts and pepper social media with dire warnings. Or I can watch them die of spiritual thirst while I stand on the sidelines shouting, "I told you so!"

But if I choose any of these, nothing will change. Those who already agree with me will applaud my efforts. But those who most need to see and hear what I'm pointing out will turn a blind eye and a deaf ear. And they won't even know it. That's what cultural blind spots do.

On the other hand, I can dam up the water so they will drink. If I genuinely want them to drink from the fresh and life-giving water of worship and God's Word, I have no other choice. I have to find a way to make it available in a way they'll drink it.

That's one reason we've designed our ministries at North Coast to provide as many worship options as possible. As I write this, we have more than fifty different worship options when you count time, day, location, and worship style. That makes it hard for the club-program parents to say they couldn't get to church. It's our attempt to sidestep and outmaneuver the scheduling conflicts and competition that the club-program culture creates. It's our way of damming up the water.

You may think our solution is genius. You may think it's crazy. That's not the point. Because it's *our* solution for *our* situation. I'd probably do something completely different if I were in your shoes or in another situation.

But I know that, as a shepherd who loves his sheep, I have to find a way to make them drink. And, yes, the way I've chosen to do so can be labeled as catering and pandering to the misplaced priorities of a consumerist and self-absorbed flock. I get that.

But until someone shows me a better option, I'll keep damming up the stream the only way I know how. Because at the end of the day, that's what a shepherd does.

CHAPTER 9

ADAPTING TO FEAR

The fears, phobias, and idiosyncrasies of individual flock members are something else that every shepherd has to deal with. Unlike cultural blind spots that tend to be nearly universal, the fears and peculiarities of individual flock members differ from person to person. They're the result of unique life experiences, family backgrounds, and innate wiring.

Sometimes they're irrational and overblown.

Sometimes they're just plain weird.

It doesn't matter. Either way they represent reality to those who struggle with them.

If we want to lead well, they can't be ignored or decried. People don't choose their fears and oddities. They're stuck with them. Most would opt out if they could. But they can't. It's not a choice they have.

IRRATIONAL FEAR

I have a friend with acrophobia. If he's anywhere near a ledge, he's terrified of falling. He knows it makes no sense. He's not in the habit of falling down. There's no reason to assume he'll suddenly lose his footing when he's within ten feet of a ledge or window.

But that doesn't matter.

After he goes past the third floor, he won't go near a window. It doesn't matter how great the view might be. It doesn't matter if the window is locked, double-paned, and shatter proof, there's no way he's going near it.

I learned long ago not to try to talk him out of his fear. It's bad for our friendship and there's nothing I can say or do that will convince him it's safe. His fear of heights is far greater than his desire to see what's going on out there.

Many in our flocks have similar irrational and paralyzing phobias in the spiritual realm. They know they should do things like boldly share their faith, study their Bibles, pray more, or give more. But they hang back, fearful, awkward, and uncertain.

Sometimes we equate their reluctance with spiritual apathy or sinful resistance. That's a mistake. There are plenty of apathetic Christians who need to have a fire lit under them. But those who hang back out of fear and insecurity are not apathetic or sinfully resistant.

It does no good to cajole, shame, or pester them to walk over to the window.

It never works.

No matter what we say or do, they will still stand with

their backs pressed against the wall. And the more we nag, the more they will cling to it. Which is why a good shepherd doesn't berate his weak, frightened, or struggling sheep. He adapts and adjusts in order to help them do what they need to do. His goal is to help the sheep, not to harangue the sheep.

As a case in point, let's consider how unfounded fears, insecurities, and personal baggage can keep many of our people from (1) sharing their faith, (2) reading their Bibles, and (3) impacting their communities, along with some of the things we can do to help them get around it.

Evangelism

Most Jesus followers know they ought to share their faith. But many don't. They're petrified of looking stupid, being rebuffed, saying the wrong thing. They're terrified of being involved in anything that resembles a debate or sales pitch.

I'm not talking about introverts. Many introverts share their faith quite boldly. I'm talking about the folks in your flock who are socially shy, insecure, or don't think well on their feet. They took an extra eight units in college to avoid a two-unit public speaking course. They're convinced their IQ drops by twenty points when they're put on the spot or have to answer probing questions.

Unfortunately, most of the evangelism training we offer in our churches scares these people to death. We equip them with canned answers to the most common questions and then ask them to strategically develop relationships with their non-Christian neighbors and coworkers, earn the right to be heard, and when the time is ripe, share the gospel.

That works great for extroverts who enjoy throwing a

block party and introverts who enjoy a deep soul-searching conversation. But to a significant subset of Jesus followers, that's a horrifying concept. It doesn't matter how many apologetic classes they take or how many answers they memorize, the moment a coworker asks them why they think the Bible is trustworthy, why a good Buddhist won't go to heaven, or why they still believe in a bunch of antiquated sexual standards, their brain cramps up.

To leaders who don't share these same fears and anxieties, this seems like foolishness. They interpret the failure of shy, passive, or socially anxious believers to aggressively engage in evangelism to be a sin issue. So instead of offering sympathy and support, they offer a rebuke. They tell these folks to get right with God, get out of their comfort zone, walk across the room, and trust the Holy Spirit to give them the right words to say.

But that's like telling my friend to get up, walk across the room, and enjoy the view.

It's not going to happen.

No matter what I do or how persistently I badger him, he's still going to stand with his back against the wall and tell me a picture will do just fine.

One way to make it easier and less threatening for these folks to share their faith without the need to eloquently explain and defend their faith is by making it easier for them to bring their non-Christian family and friends to church.

At North Coast we've opted to do everything we can to support and foster what I call "come and see" evangelism. Instead of branding those who have a hard time with evangelism as second-class Christians who aren't brave or smart enough, we've created a model that makes it easier for even our shiest and most reserved members to say, "Why don't you come and see for yourself?"

Now to be clear, I'm not talking about becoming a seeker church. I have no problem with that model, but it's not who we are. I'm simply talking about making sure the stage is set so those who struggle with explaining their faith have an opportunity to share their faith.

There are two keys to come-and-see evangelism: (1) the content has to be aimed at believers, otherwise there's nothing to come and see, and (2) everything has to be said and done in a way that those who have never been in a church before can understand everything they are watching and hearing.

To get there, we had to make a few changes.

During the early years of my ministry, I had unwittingly discouraged people from bringing their non-Christian friends. I didn't mean to. It was the last thing I wanted to do. But without realizing it, almost all of our programing, sermons, and our best attempts to be creative and clever were sending a message we never intended to send: "These meetings are for those who already know Jesus and the Bible well. Wait until we schedule a special outreach event before you bring a non-Christian friend to come and see what Jesus is all about."

For instance, in most of my sermons I referred to cross references and famous passages as if everyone in the room were familiar with them. It never dawned on me that I was subtly and subliminally screaming out that everyone here already knows the Bible well. It's no wonder no one ever brought a friend or family member who didn't know what an epistle, eschatology, pericope, or psalmist was.

Once I realized what I was doing, namely, preaching to

my seminary profs instead of the people in front of me, I started preaching and teaching as if at least 20 percent of the room were made up of window shoppers who had never been in a church before.

I didn't aim at them. But I made sure I included them.

For instance, instead of saying, "Turn to the third chapter of James," I started saying, "Turn to the right about ten pages where you'll find a letter written by a man named James," or "We're in the book of Hebrews today—you can find it listed in the table of contents."

I also stopped referring to famous biblical events as if everyone remembered or even knew them. Instead of saying, "Faith needs action. Nothing will happen until we're willing to step out of the boat," I started saying, "Faith needs action. There's a story in the Bible about a man named Peter who actually walked on the water. But only after he stepped out of the boat."

These were small changes They didn't water down our services or dumb down my sermons. No one left because they weren't being fed. But these changes sent a powerful subliminal message that there were lots of folks in the room who knew nothing about Jesus and the Bible.

And guess what?

It wasn't long until our shy and timid members started bringing friends and family who knew nothing about Jesus so they could see and hear what he's all about.

I wish more of our people were ready and eager to share their faith. But that's not the world I pastor in. So the shepherd in me found a way to dam up the water so they could drink. It beats a flock of dehydrated sheep any day.

Bible Reading

Bible reading is another thing that many of our people struggle with.

It's hard to be a Jesus follower without knowing what he said or did. That's why so many of us emphasize knowing and studying the Bible and why we want our people to become self-feeding Christians.[1]

Unfortunately, daily Bible reading doesn't work so well for those who struggle to read, have a hard time remembering what they just read, or simply dislike reading immensely.

These people are often made to feel like losers. And it's not just for not reading their Bibles. It's also for not keeping up with the latest books about the Bible. In a church culture where reading has become the quintessential tool for spiritual maturity, those who struggle with reading or simply hate to read have a hard time being taken seriously.

I have to admit, as a reader and a writer, their failure to read pains me, especially those who read well but choose not to. I wish everyone in my flock was a self-feeding Christian with a marked-up Bible and a stack of dog-eared journals at the side of his or her bed.

But that's not going to happen any time soon.

As a shepherd I don't have the luxury of being pained, frustrated, or angry. I have sheep who need to know what the Bible says so they can renew their minds and align their lives with it. It's my job to create some quiet waters so they'll drink deeply from it.

One way we've done that at North Coast is by developing a robust small-group model where all of the questions are based on the passage or passages covered in the previous weekend's sermon. There's plenty of Bible verses and content for those who read well. But for those who don't (or won't) read much, our lecture/lab model helps them interact with Scripture on multiple levels anyway.[2]

Once again, I know it would be best if everyone in my church followed a daily reading plan. But I also know many won't and some can't. As a shepherd, it's my job to make sure they are well-fed. *How* they get their spiritual nourishment is secondary to making sure they get it.

And one more thing. Before we become too frustrated with those who can but won't read their Bibles on a regular basis, we need to remember that there were rather few self-feeding Christians in the early church—or for the next fourteen centuries for that matter.

It was pretty hard to read your Bible daily until a guy named Gutenberg came along.

Community Impact

A third and final area where many of our people know what they should do but have myriad excuses why they never get around to it is community impact.

It's no news flash that many of our people gravitate toward clustering in holy huddles. They've been sent into the world, but they prefer to stay in the church.

It's nothing new. The early church did the same thing. They started in Jerusalem and decided to stay there. They ignored the Great Commission. It wasn't until the Lord allowed a great persecution to take place in Jerusalem that they finally scattered throughout Judea, Samaria, and other parts of the world.[3]

So what's a shepherd to do when the sheep only hunker down in a holy huddle?

Once again, the answer lies in adapting and adjusting to their fears and concerns, finding a way to make it easier for them to break out and engage with the world they've been called to reach.

One way we've done that is by assigning community service projects to each of our small groups. We ask them to carry out at least two service projects a year. We've found that making something an assignment helps turn a good intention into an action item.

But assigning something and helping people pull it off are two different things. And it's here I find many of us fall short. For instance, I've noticed that lots of pastors preach about the need to be missional, but they never show anyone how to do it outside of a sermon illustration or two. The fact is that most folks have no idea what to do or who to contact. So they either do nothing or end up helping out at the same soup kitchen every Thanksgiving.

To get around that problem, we've tried to create some quiet waters by not only assigning service projects but also by having a vetted list of contacts and opportunities that we keep up to date. It ensures that when a group shows up to serve, there will be something for them to do.

We also follow up to find out what was done and see how things worked out. In other words, we inspect what we expect. The truth is that lots of our groups would never move from good intentions to action if they thought we weren't going to follow up. But since they know we will be checking, they make sure they've fulfilled their obligation.

As I write this, we average more than three service projects a day in our community. That obviously has a huge impact on our schools, community organizations, and nonprofits. It also opens doors and grants us favor in the eyes of our governing authorities. And most important, it makes Jesus look good.

But none of this would ever happen if all we did was preach and harp on the importance of having a missional impact. To make it a reality, we have to dam up the waters. We have to help them paint by numbers.

It's what a good shepherd does.

He meets his sheep where they are and not where they should be.

CHAPTER 10

PURSUING THE STRAGGLER

Every spiritual leader sooner or later discovers that the story isn't over until it's over. Sinners become saints. Heroes crash and burn.

It shouldn't surprise us.

But it does.

Pretty much every time.

Early on in my pastoral ministry I made the mistake of judging too quickly. When it came to the sheep in my flock, I assumed who they were today was who they'd be forever. I should have read my Bible more closely. It's full of surprises when it comes to those who shine and those who flame out.

Peter looked like a washout. He'd failed miserably under pressure. But later he wrote parts of the Bible and courageously died a martyr's death. Who would have guessed?

Judas, on the other hand, looked like a solid choice, trustworthy enough to be appointed treasurer. When seventy-two of Jesus' disciples went out as an advance team to the towns he would visit next, they all returned rejoicing at the power they had over demonic forces. No one asked why Judas and his partner lacked miraculous power. He fit right in. There's no indication that the other apostles had any inkling that he would prove to be a wolf in sheep's clothing.[1]

Then there's Uzziah, one of the greatest kings of Judah that nobody knows about. Crowned king at just sixteen years old, he reigned for fifty-two years with Solomon-like wisdom, wealth, and military prowess. He had a great run. He sought the Lord and was greatly blessed—until he became powerful. Then his pride suddenly led to a tragic downfall. His epitaph was simply, "Here lies Uzziah, he died a leper."[2]

It's no wonder he seldom makes it into our children's Sunday school curriculum.

PATIENCE

A good shepherd needs to be patient. That's not easy. I know that from my own struggles with patience. Early on I wanted everyone in my church to be instantly mature. I loved the lost. I adored baby Christians who still swore in their prayers. I prized those who quickly raced to the front of the line. But I had no tolerance for those who lingered at the back, particularly those who kept getting out of line and wandering off into the wilderness.

For some reason, I didn't think they deserved the same kind of pursuit or forbearance that the Lord gave me. I wanted to take the stragglers behind the woodshed. I wanted to let those who kept wandering off get what they deserved—to be eaten by wolves.

I thought my impatience was Spirit-led. I thought I was helping God out by refusing to accept their lame excuses. I saw no reason to slow down and stop and chase after those who wandered off the path. Constantly searching for quiet waters or damming up the stream to make it easier for them to drink seemed like a compromising accommodation to their sin and feeble faith.

I was wrong and foolish, especially in light of Jesus' warning that he will give to me the same kind of mercy and judgment I give to others.[3]

DON'T SEAL THE BOX

What I forgot is that sanctification is a process, not an instant decision. Some sheep will move to the front of the line quickly, some will move slowly, and some will be satisfied to stay in the middle of the pack. The frustrating ones will keep wandering off over and over again.

It's a shepherd's job to care for them all. We can't play favorites.

Now that doesn't mean we should treat everyone exactly the same or that we should ignore the differences in their behavior. Only a foolish and idealistic shepherd wears blinders. Those who put their trust in liars, confide in gossips, and depend upon the undependable aren't loving and open-minded. They're dupes who will eventually pay a high price for their gullibility.

A leader has to put people into boxes. It's the only way to know how to treat them. The reality is that liars lie, helpers help, gossips gossip, the dependable show up, and the impulsive chase butterflies. A wise shepherd takes that into account and puts them into the appropriately labeled boxes.

But a good shepherd never seals the box. He knows that people change. Some for the good and some for the bad. But pretty much everybody changes over time. In order to lead well, we have to respond to who people are, not who they were.

It's here I find that many of us make a critical mistake. We're too quick to seal the boxes. When someone behaves in an unacceptable way, we pull out the box labeled uncommitted, loser, or EGR (extra grace required) and drop them into it, seal it up, and turn all of our attention to the remaining good sheep.

Yet that's not how the Lord shepherds us.

Until the day we die, he doesn't seal the box. He patiently waits for us to turn around and repent. Peter tells us that is one of the main reasons Jesus hasn't yet returned. He's waiting for more of us to change our label.

> The Lord is not slow in keeping his promise, as some understand slowness. Instead he is patient with you, not wanting anyone to perish, but everyone to come to repentance.
>
> But the day of the Lord will come like a thief. The heavens will disappear with a roar; the elements will be destroyed by fire, and the earth and everything done in it will be laid bare. (2 Peter 3:9–10)

DOGGED PURSUIT

The Lord isn't just patiently waiting for us to come around. He doggedly pursues his sheep. Even the bad ones.

The Bible says he died for us while we were his enemies. He didn't insist we clean up our act first. He didn't stand by, waiting to see if we'd cry out for help. He took the first step. He pursued us before we even knew we were lost.

Unfazed by Doubt

He also pursued a doubting and cynical apostle, showing up in midst of Thomas's doubt, not after he changed his mind and decided the reports of the resurrection were true.

He did the same when he intercepted two discouraged disciples who had given up and were headed back home to Emmaus.[4]

One More Chance

But one of my favorite examples of the way the Lord doggedly pursues his stragglers and wayward sheep is found in a passage that is too often turned on its ear by those who fail to read it carefully. They mistakenly claim that it reflects Jesus' disdain for a group of lukewarm and spiritually bankrupt believers in a city called Laodicea.

Yet that's not what the passage says. It doesn't say that Jesus detested the Laodiceans or that he had written them off or that he was disgustingly spewing them out of his mouth.

It says that he's about to do so *if* they don't repent.

His letter to the Laodiceans is not an example of Jesus' disgust at a bunch of spiritual losers. It's an example of his dogged pursuit of a bunch of spiritual losers. He's offering them still one more chance, and he ends with a plea and a promise that if they will but open the door and let him in, he will break bread with them. Notice what the passage actually says:

These are the words of the Amen, the faithful and true witness, the ruler of God's creation. I know your deeds, that you are neither cold nor hot. I wish you were either one or the other! So, because you are lukewarm—neither hot nor cold—*I am about to spit you out of my mouth.* You say, "I am rich; I have acquired wealth and do not need a thing." But you do not realize that you are wretched, pitiful, poor, blind and naked. I counsel you to buy from me gold refined in the fire, so you can become rich; and white clothes to wear, so you can cover your shameful nakedness; and salve to put on your eyes, so you can see.

Those whom I love I rebuke and discipline. So be earnest and repent. Here I am! I stand at the door and knock. If anyone hears my voice and opens the door, I will come in and eat with that person, and they with me. (Rev. 3:14–20, emphasis added)

A good shepherd will do the same. He'll pursue the straggler and wayward and care for the weakest and slowest, because that's what a shepherd does. He may have favorites, but he won't play favorites.

Now I want to be clear. We've not been talking about high-handed sin. We'll deal with that in the next chapter. Adapting to the weaknesses, failings, blind spots, and fears is not the same thing as ignoring sin in the camp. It's simply loving our flocks enough that we are willing to meet them where they are instead of waiting for them to be where they should be.

The struggling, the stragglers, and the laggards need a shepherd, not a butcher.

Because their story is never over until it's over, the fact is that some of today's worst sheep will become tomorrow's best sheep. Some will become your fellow shepherds. We just never know which ones.

Only God knows.

And he's not telling.

CHAPTER 11

FLOCK FOCUSED

As we've seen, a good shepherd adapts to the weaknesses and failings of his problematic sheep when they struggle, wander off, or otherwise can't keep up. But there's a huge difference between a *struggling* lamb and an *infectious* lamb. Those who don't understand the differences are likely to end up with either an ailing flock or no flock at all.

Struggling sheep do battle with their sins and weaknesses. Granted, they don't always seem to fight very hard, and some lose far more battles than they win, but they honestly wish it were different.

They need our help.

Infectious sheep, however, have stopped struggling. They've given up the battle. They no longer fight their sinful impulses. They defend them. They don't wish anything were different because they're convinced their sin is no big deal in the eyes of God. They're certain their situation is somehow unique or different from everyone else.

They need to be quarantined.

Unfortunately, many shepherds are hesitant to remove or quarantine toxic and infectious sheep. They fail to grasp the degree of devastation to the flock that occurs when persistent high-handed sin is ignored. They don't realize blatant sin is not only harmful but contagious—highly contagious.

There are two main reasons why we hesitate or fail to remove and quarantine toxic and infectious sheep:

1. We confuse love with looking the other way.
2. We fear collateral damage.

LOOKING THE OTHER WAY

Those who confuse love with looking the other way tend to focus almost exclusively on Jesus' incredible patience. Jesus was indeed incredibly patient. No question. We've already looked at his tenacious pursuit of the lost and his incredible forbearance.

But there is another side to that coin.

Jesus and the New Testament also exhort us to identify and separate from those who live in high-handed sin or who persist in tearing the body apart:

> If your brother or sister sins, go and point out their fault, just between the two of you. If they listen to you, you have won them over. But if they will not listen, take one or two others along, so that "every matter may be established by the testimony of two or three

witnesses." If they still refuse to listen, tell it to the church; and if they refuse to listen even to the church, treat them as you would a pagan or a tax collector. (Matt. 18:15–17)

Warn a divisive person once, and then warn them a second time. After that, have nothing to do with them. You may be sure that such people are warped and sinful; they are self-condemned. (Titus 3:10–11)

At one point the leaders in the church at Corinth fell into the trap of confusing love with looking the other way. They ignored the sin of a man who was sleeping with his father's wife.

They thought they were being loving. But the apostle Paul warned them they weren't being loving, they were being foolish. He told them they were putting the entire church in jeopardy. The cancer of the man's sin would spread like yeast in a loaf of bread if they didn't quickly remove him from the flock.[1]

THE CONTAGIOUS CONSEQUENCES OF SIN

Sin is contagious. Its consequences aren't just limited to the sinner. The body of Christ is not a theological construct. It's a reality. We are interconnected in ways that are hard for most Americans (and most anyone whose worldview is shaped by a Western European paradigm) to fathom. The persistent sin of one impacts us all.

It goes all the way back to the opening pages of the Bible.

Adam's sin still brings death to us all.[2]

The same principle brought defeat and death to the Israelite army when a man named Achan decided to take for himself a few things that belonged to God, and he hid them under his tent. It probably didn't seem like much. Just a few items no one would miss.

But in the unseen realm, it caused his entire family and all of Israel to be declared unfaithful. So much so that the conquest of the promised land came to a screeching halt. There would be no more victories until Achan's sin was dealt with. Innocent soldiers would die. Podunk towns would hold off the army of God. All because one man in the camp decided to rob God.[3]

Now I'll be the first to admit that I don't fully understand the unseen realm. I don't know why Achan's sin caused such immediate and harsh consequences. I don't know why others seem to sin with impunity for a while. But I do know that whenever the Scriptures pull back the curtain to show us the unseen realm, it reveals a powerful level of interconnectedness that is incredibly sobering, especially in the way the sins of one can impact the lives of many.

I saw this firsthand a number of years ago.

A Tale of Two Pastors

Two local pastors fell morally. In both cases it was a long-term situation that finally came to light. The sin of one quickly became public knowledge. The sin of the other pastor was carefully covered up.

I was one of only a few who knew what happened.

Unfortunately, I did not have the information, relationship, or position from which I could confront the pastor or the elders about the way they were handling the situation. When I approached them, they made it abundantly clear they did not want to talk about the issue. And since I did not have any hard evidence, I knew no one would believe me if I spoke up. So I decided to pray about it and let God deal with it in his own timing.

He did.

The truth eventually came out.

But in the meantime, while I was waiting, something very strange happened. Over the next few years I had to deal with more cases of demented and salacious sexual sin than at any other time in my ministry. It was eerie. But even stranger, in each and every case the couples involved had previously attended one of the two churches plagued by sin at the top.

Now I can understand why those who attended the church where the pastor's sins were public knowledge had a greater propensity to fall into sexual sin. After all, if he couldn't keep his pants on, why should they?

But in the case of those who had attended the church where literally no one knew what the pastor was doing behind closed doors, the only explanation was the insidious and contagious nature of sin in the unseen realm.

It's one reason I take the matter of church discipline so seriously. The Bible has a very specific list of sins a good shepherd will not ignore. While I don't want to add anything to the list and become a modern-day Pharisee with stricter standards than God himself, I also don't want to be so foolish as to assume his list of sins worthy of quarantine applies to every other flock but my own.[4]

When it comes to persistent and high-handed sin or chronic divisiveness, it's never loving to look the other way.

It's irresponsible and dangerous.

COLLATERAL DAMAGE

A second reason why some leaders fail to quarantine their diseased and infectious sheep is fear of collateral damage. They know driving out the mocker, the divisive, and those who continue in high-handed sin is seldom pain free for either the sheep or the shepherd. So they put it off until later.

Even the most toxic sheep have family and friends. They almost always lobby for another chance. They seldom agree that it's time to quarantine. And when they unite as a small army of aggrieved defenders, they can tear a flock apart.

Make no mistake, the fear of collateral damage is a *legitimate* fear. But for those who want to shepherd well, it can't become a *paralyzing* fear. The stakes are too high.

A Lesson from a Cancer Ward

Years ago my wife and I learned both the high cost of collateral damage and the reason it's worth risking it when she was diagnosed with an aggressive form of cancer. By God's grace she is fine today. But at the time, things looked bleak. The cancer appeared to have progressed rapidly, and with her particular kind of cancer, her youth lowered (rather than increased) her odds of survival.

The treatment plan with the best odds for long-term survival involved pouring harsh poisons into her in the hope they would kill off the fast-growing cancer cells. Unfortunately, back then, chemotherapy was not as narrowly targeted as it is today. We were told that the stuff they wanted to give her would kill off not just the cancer cells but also pretty much *every* fast-growing cell. She'd lose her hair, eyebrows, taste buds, and more. It would also set into motion early menopause, lifelong headaches, and a compromised immune system. In addition, they wanted to mutilate her body in order to eliminate any chance the cancer would reoccur.

For a young woman, none of that seemed like a good option. To make it all the more daunting, she felt fine. Despite the results of the biopsy, the cancer had no discernable impact on her daily life. And there were no guarantees the chemotherapy would work. All it offered was significantly better odds of *long-term* survival in exchange for a boatload of *short-term* side effects.

There were other options that were much less invasive. They avoided almost all of the collateral damage. There would be no poison and mutilation. Instead of dealing with a boatload of negative side effects, she would go through a surgical procedure, make a few lifestyle changes, and submit to an ongoing regimen of tests and observation.

The only problem was that none of these less-invasive options had anywhere near as high a survival rate for the type of cancer she had, particularly at the stage at which it was discovered. So we opted for the treatment plan with the worst side effects and the highest odds of long-term survival.

Around that same time, there were some folks we knew who chose the opposite option. They feared the harsh side effects and the collateral damage that accompanied an aggressive treatment plan. So they put it off to try something else first.

While I cannot speak to the specifics of God's leading in their lives, I can speak to the results. The cancer won. They avoided the harsh treatment and the lifelong collateral damage that my wife still faces to this day. But the price of avoidance proved to be incredibly high.

The application to leaders and shepherds is obvious. In the short run, it will almost always be less painful to put off dealing with toxic sheep. But in the long run, it will almost always cost us the rest of the flock.

Groundless Fears

Sometimes the things we fear the most have no reality. The carnage and collateral damage we dread never materializes. It was all in our heads.

I remember when North Coast was a new and struggling church plant. We had a worship leader who was a magnet and a megaphone of criticism and negativity. He always had a story about someone who was mad at me, upset, or leaving. He also had an ongoing list of things I should do differently. My stomach literally churned every time I had to talk to him.

I knew life would be better for him and for me if he moved on. But we had no one else to lead worship, and I feared if I called him out on his gossip and divisiveness and removed him from his leadership role, he'd leave the church and take all of his friends and the people whose complaints he continually passed on to me.

As the pastor of a small and dwindling flock, that seemed like a death knell.

Like many folks who are highly critical and a bad fit in their ministry role, he often voiced that perhaps it was time for him and his wife to move on. Fearing a potential backlash that would come if he exited on bad terms, I immediately moved into pastor mode. I assured him we could work it out. He agreed and then stayed on to torture me some more.

I made a critical mistake that many leaders, especially those with new or smaller ministries, make. I was praying to Jesus that he'd move my toxic nemesis on. He'd answer my prayer but then I'd sabotage his answer by talking my worship leader into staying around a little longer.

I was stupid. And I'm pretty sure Jesus wasn't too pleased.

I've since learned that when a relationally toxic lamb (especially one in a leadership role) suggests their time is up, the right thing to do is to take their keys and put them in my pocket. And after they are securely in my pocket, pastor and love on them.

Finally, one day, with the support of my elders, I took the keys.

I was certain my phone would ring off the hook.

I braced for a record low Sunday.

But to my shock nothing happened. Well, that's not exactly true. Our worship was embarrassingly bad the next Sunday and for a few months afterward. It was essentially karaoke. And bad karaoke at that. But no one (literally no one) left the church with him. In fact, only a few people even asked me where he was. Apparently, they were as fed up with his negativity as I was.

I could have kicked myself. I'd put up with nearly a year and a half of anonymous criticism, frustration, and spiritual dissonance in the unseen realm because I was afraid of collateral damage. But in reality the only damage our church suffered was the damage I inflicted by not having the guts to act sooner.

A good shepherd has the guts to do the right thing even when it's a scary thing. He doesn't stand by while the cancer spreads. He won't let one sick lamb destroy the flock. He might fear collateral damage, but he's not paralyzed by it. He knows that cancer kills in the long run. So he cuts it out before it spreads too far.

SECTION 3
SERVE WITH ENTHUSIASM

Be shepherds of God's flock that is under your care,
watching over them—not because you must, but
because you are willing, as God wants you to be;
not pursuing dishonest gain, but eager to serve.

—1 PETER 5:2

CHAPTER 12

PRIVILEGED TO SERVE

The gospel is not just good news. It's inconceivably good news that turns death-row rebels into sons and daughters of God. It gives reprobates in desperate need of a stay of execution a full pardon, a new identity, and a glorious, imperishable inheritance.

Even more astounding, it entrusts some of us with the incredible privilege of shepherding God's flock, caring for his prized possession. But if we aren't careful we can lose our sense of awe at what God has done and what he allows us to do. We can begin to see our great privilege as a harsh burden.

Perhaps that's why Peter was careful to exhort his fellow shepherds to serve enthusiastically, willingly and eagerly embracing the privilege of spiritual leadership:

> Be shepherds of God's flock that is under your care, watching over them—not because you must, but because you are willing, as God wants you to be; not pursuing dishonest gain, but eager to serve. (1 Peter 5:2)

WHEN THE THRILL IS GONE

Over the years I've had the honor of mentoring and training thousands of pastors and spiritual leaders. Most love what they do. But occasionally I encounter a leader or a pastor who longs to do something else. The thrill is gone. In some cases, it was never there. They shepherd and lead out of obligation. They're beaten down, emotionally depleted, trapped in a role they wish they could abandon.

Sometimes it's merely a rough patch they need to power through. At other times it's because they've been running too hard for too long. They need a break to step back, replenish, and refocus. But in some cases, the malaise continues. Nothing helps. Even after taking time away to refresh and refocus, they still find themselves leading out of a sense of obligation, begrudgingly instead of willingly and eagerly.

At that point, I usually suggest something that shocks them. I urge them to quit.

More often than not, they look at me as if I've also asked them to renounce their faith.

That's because they've confused leadership with discipleship. They've never considered quitting their leadership role as a viable option. They've fantasized about it. But they felt guilty for doing so. The idea of abandoning their leadership role strikes them as the ultimate spiritual capitulation. They can't imagine how Jesus would be pleased with them.

It's a common mistake.

DISCIPLESHIP AND LEADERSHIP ARE TWO DIFFERENT THINGS

I grew up in a ministry context where there were two primary goals at every summer camp, missions conference, or revival: (1) save the lost and (2) garner commitments to the mission field or some other form of full-time ministry.

They assumed that leadership (especially vocational ministry) was the ultimate rung on the discipleship ladder, the highest form of spiritual commitment. They didn't understand that discipleship and leadership are two different things. Discipleship is a requirement for all; leadership is a calling for some.

Not much has changed.

For example, recently I was talking to some college students who had been deeply involved in a campus ministry while pursuing their degrees. They'd served in a leadership capacity, so, with graduation looming, they were approached by the staff of the parachurch ministry they'd been involved in and were asked to consider raising support in order to join the ministry on a full-time basis.

There's nothing wrong with that.

But then the hard-sell pressure began. They were told that they would be "wasting their life" if they pursued a career in the fields they'd studied for. If they were serious about Jesus and the kingdom, there was only one logical option: they needed to abandon their career path, raise support, and join the team. Anything else was a spiritual compromise, a pursuit of temporal things instead of eternal things.

I ran into the same mind-set when I decided to become a pastor. It was obvious that a lot of folks in my church and at the college I attended were quite pleased I'd made such a meritorious choice. Somehow, I was suddenly a more committed and better Christian.

With pressure and paradigms like that, it's no wonder so few shepherds and leaders think of stepping back or stepping down as a viable alternative, no matter how miserable or ineffective they may be.

When leadership is seen as the endgame of discipleship, quitting is simply not an option.

A CHOICE, NOT A REQUIREMENT

When Paul wrote to Timothy and gave instructions for leading the church in Ephesus, he included a set of qualifications for leaders. Unfortunately, we tend to overlook his introduction to the list. It includes an important qualifier: "Here is a trustworthy saying: Whoever *aspires* to be an overseer desires a noble task" (1 Tim. 3:1, emphasis added).

Don't miss this. Paul didn't tell Timothy to persuade everyone to become a leader. He told him to vet those who *aspired* to become leaders. That's a rather significant difference.

It's the same with Jesus' call to servant leadership. We tend to apply it to everyone. But it wasn't addressed to everyone. It was addressed to those who *wanted* to hold the highest positions of leadership in his kingdom:

> Jesus called them together and said, "You know that the rulers of the Gentiles lord it over them, and their high officials

exercise authority over them. Not so with you. Instead, whoever wants to become great among you must be your servant, and whoever wants to be first must be your slave—just as the Son of Man did not come to be served, but to serve, and to give his life as a ransom for many." (Matt. 20:25–28)

We are all called to love others and to put their needs and interests above our own. But servant leadership is a choice. It's the pathway of promotion for those who want to advance to higher positions of leadership in the kingdom. But it's not the path for everyone.[1]

Unfortunately, when leadership becomes the preferred endgame for anyone who seriously pursues discipleship, we inevitably end up with leaders who serve out of obligation rather than calling, and that does a great disservice to both the begrudging shepherd and the flock.

None of this is meant to say that finding, equipping, and deploying leaders is an unimportant task. It's an incredibly important task. A leader who doesn't produce other leaders is just a tour guide. Without reproduction, everything dies. That's why Paul told Timothy to make reproducing leaders a top priority. But developing leaders is not the same thing as trying to turn everyone into a leader or assuming that everyone can and should become a leader.[2]

GIFT PROJECTION

One of the reasons leadership and vocational ministry tend to be lifted up as a higher calling is our propensity toward gift projection, that is, the natural tendency we all have to project our personal calling and giftedness onto everyone else. It helps to explain why so many shepherds try to turn every lamb into a leader. We assume our personal path of discipleship and obedience is the only path of discipleship and obedience.

But the fact is that many of God's sheep have no desire to lead. Their two favorite verses are found in Paul's first letter to the Thessalonians:

> Make it your ambition to lead a quiet life: You should mind your own business and work with your hands, just as we told you, so that your daily life may win the respect of outsiders and so that you will not be dependent on anybody. (1 Thess. 4:11–12)

For many leaders, it's hard to believe such a passage is actually in the Bible.

THE PRIESTHOOD OF BELIEVERS

A misunderstanding of the biblical concept of ministry is another reason we end up with shepherds and leaders who serve out of obligation rather than willingly and eagerly.

For instance, I'm often asked if any of my kids are in ministry.

I always say, "Yes, all three. And better yet, they all serve with me at North Coast."

"What do they do?"

"One is a business executive, one is a schoolteacher, and the other works for a government contractor and dabbles in real estate."

Inevitably, that elicits a puzzled look. They're wondering what kind of strange church has a staff like that.

Then I say, "Oh, I'm sorry. You meant *vocational* ministry. All of my kids are in ministry. But none of them are paid for it."

Every Christian is called into ministry. It's not something for a select few. The moment we step over the line and become a Jesus follower, we're in the ministry. The only question is where we're supposed to serve him. Paul put it this way: "Whatever you do, whether in word or deed, do it all in the name of the Lord Jesus, giving thanks to God the Father through him" (Col. 3:17).

To do everything in the name of the Lord Jesus simply means to speak and act as his representative. In essence, we've all been assigned the role of a key spokesman or the role of an ambassador to represent, speak, and act for him in every situation.

Unfortunately, whenever ministry becomes something delegated to a select few highly committed Jesus followers who are supposedly "called" to serve Jesus on a "full-time" basis, it relegates everyone else to the sidelines. It undercuts the priesthood of believers, one of the most important doctrines in the New Testament.

It's no wonder we end up with missionaries and pastors who feel like misfits. They're playing out of position. They were never called nor empowered for the role they're trying to fulfill.

FRONTLINE MINISTRY

The frontline ministry carried out in the marketplace is actually more important than the church-based ministry carried out by those of us in vocational ministry. The front lines are where the battles are won and lost.

If you don't believe me, consider what happened in China and Western Europe.

All of the missionaries and pastors in China were expelled or imprisoned soon after the rise of the Communists. Meanwhile, the church in Western Europe enjoyed complete freedom of religion and a highly educated and trained professional clergy. At first glance, that seemed like a great spiritual tragedy for China and a wonderful blessing for Western Europe. But time proved this to be the exact opposite.

The removal of the professional ministry class didn't destroy the church in China; it unleashed the latent and previously suppressed power of the laity, which led to explosive growth despite terrible persecution and the need to go underground.

Meanwhile the church in Europe suffered steep decline as everyone sat back and waited for the professionals to do the work of ministry.

That's why those who step back from a leadership role are not second-class disciples. They're simply transferring to the incredibly important front lines where they will serve Jesus on special assignment in the setting, neighborhood, or career he calls them to.

A CASE STUDY

A number of years ago I had lunch with a man I'll call Aaron. He was an A+ layman. He represented Jesus well in the marketplace and effectively shared his faith with coworkers and friends on a regular basis. He also had a knack for making money and a gift for giving it away. It was his primary spiritual gift, and he used it to fund a ton of ministries.[3]

But he felt like a spiritual failure.

He had an old-school ministry paradigm and was haunted by the story of the rich young ruler. He was sure the only way to be fully committed to Jesus was to give up his career and become a missionary or a pastor.

He wanted to meet with me so I could help him decide which path to take. Should he go to seminary in order to become a pastor or should he go straight to the mission field instead?

It was an awkward conversation. The truth was, he wasn't cut out for either one. He was far too independent to be an effective team member on a church staff or the mission field. And he was far too impatient to be a team leader. He'd made all of his money as a deal maker. He worked solo, intuitively jumping on opportunities as they came along.

Even worse, he had no skills as a communicator. He effectively shared his faith one on one; however, when it came to communicating to a group, even a small one, he was terminally boring. But of course, everyone always told him that it was great. They were trying to encourage him. He thought they were being honest.

Aaron is a perfect case study of what happens when we elevate vocational ministry and positions of leadership over marketplace ministry. Those on the front lines are devalued and subtly enticed to leave their calling for a role Jesus neither equipped nor called them to fulfill.

WILLING AND DISCOURAGED

This doesn't mean those of us who are genuinely called to shepherd and lead will never feel like giving up. Confusion, frustration, and seasons of discouragement are par for the course when it comes to leadership. There's no need to bail out at the first sign of despair.

Even Jesus hit the wall and asked for a reprieve.[4]

The apostle Paul was depressed. At one point he felt as though his burden was too great to bear. That's why he penned these words:

> We do not want you to be uninformed, brothers and sisters, about the troubles we experienced in the province of Asia. We were under great pressure, far beyond our ability to endure, so that we despaired of life itself. Indeed, we felt we had received the sentence of death. But this happened that we might not rely on ourselves but on God, who raises the dead. (2 Cor. 1:8–9)

The most telling difference between shepherds who are called and gifted to lead and those who serve out of guilt and obligation is their response to the failures, hardships, and discouragements of leadership. Those who have a genuine call also have a God-given passion for the task.

Even in the darkest of days, the Spirit compels them to keep after it. They may face a season of despair. They may wonder if they can keep on going. But deep down inside, they know they can't quit. It's not a sense of guilt. It's not because they worry what others will think. It's because it's who they are. It's who God made them to be. They can't help but lead.

It's much like the passion that keeps a marathoner running, a PhD student studying, and a world-class mountaineer climbing. They all willingly and eagerly endure all kinds of rigors in their pursuit of the prize that the rest of us would walk away from. It's not that they enjoy the pain or the struggle. It's that they consider the reward to be well worth it.

If that's you, keep after it. You'll eventually hear, "Well done, good and faithful servant."

But if that's not you, don't despair. You're not stuck with a lifetime sentence. You have a choice. If your leadership role has become a burdensome obligation, it's okay to take a break or serve Jesus elsewhere.

Go do something else.

Jesus won't be disappointed with you. You'll still hear, "Well done, good and faithful servant."

CHAPTER 13

THE NO COMPLAINING RULE

If a corporate executive bemoans the declining quality of service in the first-class cabin of his favorite airline he gets little sympathy. Same for an NBA superstar who grumbles about his arduous travel schedule. They come off as ungrateful and sadly out of touch.

In much the same way, the angels must shake their heads in befuddlement when those of us who are spiritual shepherds have lost our enthusiasm and only serve out of obligation, complaining about the hardships and difficulties that come with spiritual leadership. We've been granted an incredible privilege, especially those of us who make a living at it. We're living the dream. No one put a gun to our heads. Yet to hear some shepherds talk, you'd think we've been given the short end of the stick.

The quest to accomplish anything of significance always comes at a high price. The mountaineer who wants to conquer the world's great summits has to endure harsh conditions and physical exhaustion. It's part of the process. It's what separates him from those who settle for an occasional summer evening walk in the neighborhood. He doesn't complain about the hardships. He embraces them.

Same for the gymnast who dreams of competing in the Olympics. She doesn't protest her demanding training schedule. She knows that's what she signed up for. If she hates it and constantly complains about it, her coach will tell her to become an ex-gymnast.

It's no different for those of us who serve as spiritual shepherds. The long hours, the hardships, the crushing stress, the unfair criticism, the staunch resistance, the misunderstanding that we may have to endure along the way are not unique to spiritual leadership. They're the price every leader pays, no matter what the arena. If we can't accept and embrace the pain, we need to do something else.

Complaining is not an option.

At least not a good one.

GRUMBLING IS NEVER A GOOD IDEA

No matter how tough things might get, complaining never makes things better. In the spiritual realm, it always makes them worse.

The Bible is replete with examples of people who grumbled and paid a high price for it. Consider what happened to the Israelites as they left Egypt and headed for the promised land. They had some legit things to complain about; being penned in by mountains on both sides with a large body of water in front and a superior army attacking from behind is hardly an ideal place to set up camp. Who wouldn't be bummed out at being stuck in the desert without water or food? But even filet mignon and lobster get old after a while. I can understand their growing dissatisfaction with manna.

But their grumbling and complaining didn't fix anything. It never does. It simply skews our perspective, pushing our past blessings and provisions to the background while magnifying our current hardships and deprivations. Like the Israelites, we end up longing for the leeks and onions of Egypt but forgetting the beatings and slavery that came with them:

> We remember the fish we ate in Egypt at no cost—also the cucumbers, melons, leeks, onions and garlic. But now we have lost our appetite; we never see anything but this manna! (Num. 11:5–6)

Think about that. Their grumbling eventually escalated to the point they actually began to believe the fish and food they ate in Egypt came at "no cost."

It was free.

Abundant.

There for the taking.

Now I don't know about you, but I hardly consider four hundred years of bitter slavery and forced labor to be free. To my thinking, that's a rather high price to pay. But that's what happens when we complain. It blinds us to reality. It puts the spotlight on what we lack and a veil over what we have.

That's why I believe those of us who are privileged to

lead any part of God's flock need to institute a strict No Complaining Rule.

GOD'S WILL AND THE NO COMPLAINING RULE

Whenever it comes time to make a major decision, most of us seek wise counsel and do everything we can to discover God's will. But the fact is that in many of the areas where we agonize most, he doesn't care all that much. We have lots of freedom.

For example, we often seek to discover where he wants us to live or work. We tend to think that if we can find the right neighborhood or land the right job, everything will work out perfectly. But in most cases, God doesn't care all that much. He's far more concerned with *how* we live and work than *where* we live and work.

But there is one aspect of God's will he has made abundantly clear: he wants us to be thankful, no matter what the circumstances. He wants us to "rejoice always, pray continually, give thanks in all circumstances; for this is God's will for you in Christ Jesus" (1 Thess. 5:16–18).

It's not because God needs his ego stroked. It's because we need to constantly be reminded of our blessings in order to maintain perspective. We all tend to lose it rather quickly. But when we focus on what is praiseworthy instead of what we wish was different, it brings the kindness of God back into focus. It fuels our faith, because it's always much easier to trust God when we remember what he's already done instead of focusing on what he hasn't yet done.

Complaining doesn't just skew our perspective, it actually puts us at odds with God:

> Now these things occurred as examples to keep us from setting our hearts on evil things as they did. Do not be idolaters, as some of them were; as it is written: "The people sat down to eat and drink and got up to indulge in revelry." We should not commit sexual immorality, as some of them did—and in one day twenty-three thousand of them died. We should not test Christ, as some of them did—and were killed by snakes. And do not grumble, as some of them did—and were killed by the destroying angel. (1 Cor. 10:6–10)

Obviously, that should quash all grumbling. According to this passage, God included the story of the Israelites' grumbling and his stern response to it, not so we could have some cool stories to teach our kids in Sunday school, but to scare the complaining out of us. It's another reason why those of us in spiritual leadership need to institute a strict No Complaining Rule.

PRAYER

Now I'm not suggesting we have to love everything that happens to us or that it's somehow wrong to want things to change. We need to be thankful *in* all things. But that doesn't mean we have to be thankful *for* all things. Otherwise, prayer makes no sense.

By definition, intercessory and persistent prayers are complaints against the status quo. We're asking God to change something we don't like about the current state of affairs. And that's exactly how Jesus taught us to pray, with persistence and passion.[1]

But it's one thing to complain *to* God and it's another to grumble and complain *about* God and the task or situation he's called or placed us into.

AVOID THE ECHO CHAMBER

Years ago I attended a conference where a well-known and highly successful pastor stood up and proclaimed the unique challenges of ministry. We all left feeling like we were incredibly important, had one of the most difficult jobs in the world, and had bull's-eyes painted on our backs that the Devil was constantly aiming at.

I came home and asked our elders to put together a prayer team to pray for me and our pastors. I explained that we pastors and missionaries had it particularly rough. Our job was the most difficult and dangerous job out there.

As I was waxing eloquent, one of the elders leaned forward. It was not a good lean. It was the forward lean of a man ready to leap out of his seat and punch me out.

In an instant I knew what he was thinking.

I realized I had spoken like a fool.

The elder was a retired marine who had served three tours of duty in Vietnam. He'd been drafted; he hadn't signed up. He'd had no choice. He'd watched friends die. He'd seen and experienced the kinds of atrocities I had only read about and averted my eyes whenever they were portrayed in a movie.

He was ambushed.

I've suffered the horrible indignity of friends leaving the church.

He was shot at.

I've had awful and slanderous things said about me on social media.

He wondered if he'd ever see his wife and kids again.

I've worried if we'd make the budget.

You get the point.

Make no mistake. Spiritual leadership is a difficult task. But it is not uniquely difficult or challenging. Every garden has its weeds. It's been that way since the fall.

If you're a shepherd, I warn you to beware of the ministry echo chamber. It tells us what we want to hear. It seldom tells us the truth. It perpetuates the myth that missionaries, pastors, and shepherds have the hardest jobs out there. It's a myth widely proclaimed at conferences, Bible schools, and seminaries by pastors, missionaries, and professors who believe it because they've never had a real job in their lives.

ISN'T THIS WHAT WE SIGNED UP FOR?

Ironically, the most common complaint I hear from my fellow shepherds is that their flocks treat them like on-call servants.

Yet isn't that what we signed up for?

Isn't that what Jesus called us to be?

Someone told me years ago, "If you don't want to pick

up poop, don't get a dog. And if you don't want to be taken advantage of, don't sign up for leadership."

It was good advice.

The demeaning and frustrating parts of spiritual leadership are not something to complain about; they're something to embrace, especially in light of the prize set before us. As a pastor, I get paid for doing what I used to do for free in my spare time. I bet many of you are in the same boat. So let's stop complaining and start following the wise advice a fellow shepherd once wrote from a Roman prison cell:

> Finally, brothers and sisters, whatever is true, whatever is noble, whatever is right, whatever is pure, whatever is lovely, whatever is admirable—if anything is excellent or praiseworthy—think about such things. Whatever you have learned or received or heard from me, or seen in me—put it into practice. And the God of peace will be with you. (Phil. 4:8–9)

(By the way, don't tell my elder board that I used to happily do this for free.)

SECTION 4
LEAD BY EXAMPLE

Not lording it over those entrusted to you,
but being examples to the flock.

—1 PETER 5:3

CHAPTER 14

SERVANT LEADERS

When it comes to leadership, there are several paths to success. Some leaders bark out orders. Others seek buy-in. Some use fear and intimidation. Some depend on position and protocol. Still others swear by the power of collaboration.

But when it comes to leading like a shepherd, we've seen that the first two exhortations based on Peter's appeal (1 Peter 5:1–4)—thinking like a shepherd and serving with enthusiasm—are pointing us in a very different direction to becoming a successful leader. The path becomes even more unique when we consider Peter's third admonition—*lead by example.* Jesus not only rejects all forms of leadership that depend upon fear, intimidation, or strict protocol, but presents himself as the perfect example of a new kind of leader, the *servant leader*:

> The rulers of the Gentiles lord it over them, and their
> high officials exercise authority over them. Not so with

you. Instead, whoever wants to become great among you must be your servant, and whoever wants to be first must be your slave—just as the Son of Man did not come to be served, but to serve, and to give his life as a ransom for many. (Matt. 20:25–28)

Unfortunately, some Christians have defined "lording it over" as anything that smacks of strong, forceful leadership. They cry foul any time a leader assertively sets the agenda, gives out directives, or holds them accountable. They mistakenly equate servant leadership with abdicated leadership. They want a counselor, not a leader.

JESUS WASN'T SOFT

Jesus was the quintessential servant leader. But no one would call him soft. He said and demanded hard things, sometimes rather gruffly. His inner circle periodically asked him to lighten up. They thought he was unnecessarily thinning the herd and offending those in authority. The idea that he was everybody's best friend is a romanticized and idealized myth that has no grounding in Scripture. The religious establishment considered him to be rude and condescending. They felt threatened. That's one of the reasons they turned on him.[1]

He clearly wasn't Mr. Rogers in a beard.

What makes someone a servant leader is not a lack of spunk or authority. It's a laser-like focus on meeting the needs of others.

Servant leaders are dialed in on what's best for the people

they lead, not for themselves. They seldom keep score. And if they do, they play to lose. They don't complain, quit, or walk away when the scoreboard shows they're way behind, giving up more than they're getting. They realize that's how servanthood works.

But make no mistake. Servant leaders still lead. They don't take a poll to find out where the sheep want to go. They don't crowdsource their vision. They always put the Father's agenda above the flock's agenda, even when no one appreciates or understands what they're up to.

PERKS AND PRIVILEGES

I've also noticed servant leaders have a completely different take on the perks and privileges of leadership than those who lord it over their flocks.

Those who lord it over others tend to revel in and demand the symbols and trappings of authority. It's one of the most obvious and telling signs that a leader cares more for himself than the flock. They love the perks and privileges.

Whenever I run into someone who insists upon being introduced, addressed, or pampered in a way that calls attention to their status, role, or educational pedigree, I know I'm in the presence of someone who leads by fear, intimidation, or protocol. They may talk or preach about servant leadership, but it's obvious they have no idea what it actually is. Their focus on the symbols of authority and status gives them away.

It reminds me of a lunch meeting I had with a group of pastors a number of years ago. When we went around the table and introduced ourselves, we all used our first names. That is, everyone except Dr. Insecurity. He pointedly introduced himself as Dr. Insecurity, making it clear that he didn't have a first name that peons like us were allowed to use in public.

What he didn't know was that everyone else at the table had earned doctorates of their own. No one said anything. We just went on with the meal, making sure to address him properly each time he was brought into the conversation.

But afterward a few of us set up a pool to wager on how long he'd last at his new church. The guy who picked eighteen months won. I'd put my money on twelve.

Servant leaders don't relish or demand the symbols of authority. They don't find their identity in a seat at the head table, a proper introduction, a palatial office, preferred parking, or any of the other accoutrements that come with positions of power and authority. They can accept the perks and privileges of leadership when they're appropriate. But they neither need nor demand them.

Servant leaders find their ultimate joy and status in helping others. They don't care who gets the credit or the perks. They don't sulk when their contribution is overlooked or taken for granted. They're happy to see their fruit growing on someone else's tree. And they willingly wash the feet of others. They don't wait for someone lower on the food chain to wash theirs.

THE CURSE OF INSECURITY

I've come to believe that insecurity is the greatest hindrance to servant leadership. Insecure leaders can't humbly serve others because anything that fails to support their power and status picks at the scab of their self-doubt. They can take on the role of serving others and do things that look like they are putting others first, but only so long as everyone knows that it's a role they're playing, that they're not *really* a servant.

Secure leaders, on the other hand, are comfortable in their own skin. They know who they are without the need to constantly remind everyone else who's boss. They find their identity in Jesus, not the praise of others.

Secure leaders are a lot like emotionally healthy parents who change dirty diapers, get up in the middle of the night, and willingly adjust their entire lives and schedules around the needs of their children. They don't feel shamed or devalued by their servant role (some would say slave role). It's what parents do.

In the same way, leaders who fully grasp their identity in Christ can do things and put up with slights an insecure leader can't handle. They don't feel belittled or demeaned when they have to change some proverbial diapers, are taken for granted, or forced to endure any of the more humbling aspects of servant leadership. They see it as a sign of strength, not weakness.

IT STARTS WITH OUR IDENTITY

There are two stories in the Bible that illustrate the contrasting empowerment that comes with a secure identity and the self-sabotaging poison of insecurity.

When the apostle John tells the story of Jesus' washing

feet, he sets the stage by taking us into the mind of Jesus, letting us know exactly what he was thinking as he took the basin, picked up a towel, and knelt down to wash the feet of his apostles:

> Jesus knew that the Father had put all things under his power, and that he had come from God and was returning to God; so he got up from the meal, took off his outer clothing, and wrapped a towel around his waist. After that, he poured water into a basin and began to wash his disciples' feet, drying them with the towel that was wrapped around him. (John 13:3–5)

Notice that Jesus (1) knew the Father had put all things under his power, (2) knew that he had come from God, and (3) knew he was returning to God.

That's a rather strong and clear sense of identity, security, and destiny. No wonder he could take on the role of the lowest servant. Unlike everyone else in the room, he had nothing to prove and no one to impress.

A contrasting story of an insecure and failed leader is found in 1 Kings where the sad story of a young wannabe king is chronicled. Rehoboam was the son of the great King Solomon. To say the least, he had a lot going for him.

After Solomon died, just days before Rehoboam's coronation, he was met by a delegation of Israelites asking him to lighten the heavy load of taxation and forced labor that his father had put upon them.

His older advisors told him to comply with their request, alleviating their financial burden instead of filling his already overflowing royal coffers. They told him, "If today you will be a servant to these people and serve them and give them a favorable answer, they will always be your servants" (1 Kings 12:7).

But Rehoboam couldn't do it. He was too insecure. He feared that it would make him look weak. So after consulting with and listening to his young friends, he told the delegation, "My little finger is thicker than my father's waist. My father laid on you a heavy yoke; I will make it even heavier. My father scourged you with whips; I will scourge you with scorpions" (1 Kings 12:10–12).

My bet is that he went to bed that night feeling rather smug.

He'd showed them who was the boss.

They'd learned their lesson.

But a mere three days later he woke up to find he was a king without much of a kingdom. All of the Israelites except those who lived in Judah had left him and installed another king who promised to lighten their load. It had taken Rehoboam less than a week to squander the massive kingdom and powerful throne his father had left him.

Ironically, he should have known better. His dad had written down the secret to a long and prosperous reign in a book we know as Proverbs:

> Love and faithfulness keep a king safe;
>> through love his throne is made secure. (20:28)

It's a rather simple recipe: put the needs and interests of others above your own and keep your promises. For those who are secure in their identity and destiny, it's not that hard to do. But for those who are saddled with the curse of insecurity and the need to show everyone who's the boss, king, or shepherd, it's almost impossible to pull off.

Just ask Rehoboam.

CHAPTER 15

SHEPHERDS AND COWBOYS

It's not just a laser-like focus on serving others that sets shepherd leaders apart. It's also the manner in which they lead. They don't just give orders. They set an example. It's the biblical model.

JESUS, PAUL, PETER, AND THE PHARISEES

Jesus laid down plenty of commands. But his call to discipleship was "follow me," not "listen to me." He didn't ask his disciples to do anything he wasn't already doing himself. He led by example.

Consider the way he motivated and taught them to pray. He didn't start out with a lecture series on the importance of prayer. He didn't prod them to pray more. He simply prayed. He regularly got up early and headed off into the wilderness to spend significant time with his heavenly Father.

Then one day, after he'd finished praying, one of his disciples came up and asked him to teach them to pray. It was then (in a teachable moment produced by his consistent example) that he gave them a template of things to pray about. It's what we now call the Lord's Prayer.[1]

It was the same with the apostle Paul. He wasn't shy about telling his flock what to do. He wrote lots of memos and gave plenty of commands. We call them epistles. But he summed up his leadership style in one simple command: "Follow my example, as I follow the example of Christ" (1 Cor. 11:1).

The apostle Peter also emphasized the importance of leading by example when he commanded those of us who shepherd God's flock not to lord it over those entrusted to us but to be an example to the flock.[2]

Then there were the Pharisees, the self-important and failed religious leaders of Jesus' day. They were the mirror opposite of Jesus. They didn't set an example. They gave orders, often demanding their disciples to do things they were no longer willing to do. Worse, they were loath to lift a finger to help anyone carry out their arduous demands. They were the ultimate example of leading from behind with commands and directives.[3]

DON'T PUSH THE STRING

The problem with leading from behind with commands and directives is that it seldom works for very long. It might appear to work for a while. But eventually it makes a mess of everything.

Dwight Eisenhower, one of the great leaders of the last century, understood this clearly. He rose to the highest levels in both the military and civilian realm, leading the Allied troops to victory in World War II and elected to two terms as president of the United States.

He was a strong proponent of leading from the front, setting an example to follow rather than barking out orders from the back of the pack. To illustrate the power of leading by example, he would often place a string or chain at one end of a table and then ask those in attendance what would happen if he tried to push it to the other end of the table.

The correct answer was, "There's no way to know." Because each section of the string or link in the chain would respond differently, taking the path of least resistance. And once he got it to the other side of the table, it would inevitably be bunched up in a tangled mess.

Then he'd ask what would happen if rather than *pushing* the string or chain where he wanted it to go, he instead grabbed an end of it and *pulled* it wherever he wanted it to go. He'd then point out that it would follow him wherever he wanted it to go, and once it got there, there would be no need to untangle a gnarly mess.

Without realizing it, Eisenhower was advocating a New Testament leadership model. He was describing the way ancient and modern-day shepherds lead their flocks. They lead them from the front. They set an example. They don't stand in the back and shout out orders.

Unfortunately, a lot of modern-day spiritual shepherds no longer lead like a shepherd. They lead like a CEO, an entrepreneur, a commandant. They lead their flocks more like cowboys than shepherds. And in one sense, I get it. Cowboys are a lot more glamorous than shepherds.

SHEPHERDS OR COWBOYS?

The cowboy is an American icon, romanticized in literature and cinema. He sits tall in the saddle, a man of few words, oozing testosterone and confidence. He's not to be messed with by man or beast.

Shepherds? Not so much. I can't think of a single movie or novel glamorizing a shepherd's life. Can you?

As we've seen, they've long been considered social outcasts and losers. That's the main reason why the story of the angels announcing Jesus' birth to a bunch of shepherds out in the fields was such a big deal. Luke included it in his gospel because they epitomized the kind of people Jesus came for and they were the last group of people anybody would have entrusted with a press release.

Yet despite their lowly status, the Bible consistently portrays them as the ideal metaphor for spiritual leadership. The Lord himself is portrayed as our Great Shepherd. David and Moses were tasked with shepherding God's flock. And those of us who take on the mantle of spiritual leadership are called first and foremost to be shepherds. Not generals. Not CEOs. Not visionaries. Not entrepreneurs. Not cowboys.

Just shepherds.

So what's the difference? There are many. But here are three major areas where the leadership style of a shepherd is radically different from a cowboy.

Relationship Based

A shepherd leads his sheep.

A cowboy drives his cattle.

Sheep know the shepherd's voice. They won't follow the voice of another. When he walks in front, they willingly follow out of a relationship built of trust and care.

A cowboy harasses and prods his cattle from behind. He cracks a whip and yells a lot. He controls his herd with fear and intimidation. There's no relationship. It's a one-and-done journey to the slaughterhouse.

To be fair, fear-based leadership is a model that works well in the short run. It produces high levels of compliance and performance—as long as the leader remains strong and powerful. But the moment a fear-based leader turns aside or takes a break, the cattle drive stalls. Everyone heads off in their own direction. Worse, at the first sign of weakness or vulnerability, a fear-based leader is doomed. No one comes to the aid of a struggling despot. They pile on. They get even. Then they rush to anoint a new king. Because as we saw in the case of Rehoboam, without love, a throne is never secure.

A Measured Pace

A shepherd leads at a measured pace.

A cowboy's pace is frenzied and chaotic.

A shepherd walks his flock to its destination. There's no rush. Even his sheep dogs are bred and trained to be forceful but gentle. The goal is to get them where they need to go without stressing them out too much.

A cowboy's pace is a race against the clock. He can't drive them so fast that they lose marketable weight, but he needs to get them to market as soon as possible. So cowhands on horseback bark out orders and herding dogs nip at the heels of the wayward or slow-moving heifers. No one cares if the herd is stressed out. They'll be dead soon anyway.

Just as a cowboy has little patience with the laggards, so, too, cowboy-like spiritual leaders have little patience with their flocks. They expect major life changes overnight. They think the weak and struggling need to be prodded and pushed harder, not coddled. And they think they're helping out God by hurrying everyone along.

Shepherd-like spiritual leaders take their cues from Jesus. They're filled with compassion and concern for the weak and burdened. They offer help, rest, and a lighter load; not a tongue-lashing or a spiritual beatdown.

Jesus said, "Come to me, all you who are weary and burdened, and I will give you rest. Take my yoke upon you and learn from me, for I am gentle and humble in heart, and you will find rest for your souls" (Matt. 11:28–29).

That's not something a cowboy would ever think of offering a straggling cow.

Known and Pursued

A shepherd knows his sheep and pursues those that wander off.[4]

To a cowboy, a cow is just a number with a brand and a price tag.

A shepherd quickly realizes if one of his lambs is missing. He'll immediately put the rest of the flock in the pen while he goes off to search for it.

If a cow gets lost or left behind, a cowboy keeps on going.

It's a big deal and a significant financial loss, but the drive must go on. There's no time to turn back to retrieve the lost or straggling. The marketplace window won't stay open that long.

NUMBERS OR FACES?

I've notice that when a ministry or church grows to the point of more than a few hundred people, most pastors and leaders become more like cowboys. We stop focusing on *who* shows up and start focusing on *how many* show up.

Usually it's because we see no other option. We're overwhelmed. We have too many sheep to monitor individually, so we settle for counting the sheep.

But the problem with tracking numbers is that numbers lie. They never tell the whole story.

For example, if attendance at your church increased by fifty people from one month to the next, you'd probably be thrilled. But what if a closer look at the faces in the room revealed that one hundred new people had walked through the front door—and fifty others had wandered out the back door unnoticed?

That wouldn't be cause for celebration.

That would be cause for concern.

Grave concern.

But in most churches, no one notices who walks out the back door as long as total attendance is increasing. It's not until someone asks if anyone has seen the Brandts or the Hoffmans recently that anyone notices—and by then, they've usually been gone for months.

Whenever I point this out, I'm often told that it's impractical and unrealistic to expect a larger ministry to keep track of every individual. And in one sense, they're right. The larger the ministry, the harder it is to know who's who. There's no way any one shepherd can personally know and keep track of that many people. But that doesn't mean it's impossible or no longer important. It simply means we have to develop and institute new structures, policies, and procedures to find a way to get the job done. Because when something is important, there's always a way.

WHAT'S MOST IMPORTANT?

To drive this point home, I often ask a room full of church leaders how many of their churches collect an offering of some sort.

They all raise their hands.

"How accurately do you count the money?"

"To the penny," they tell me.

"Do you send your donors an IRS receipt at the end of the year?"

"Of course."

"How accurate are they?"

"To the penny."

"So you track and connect every penny to the donor it came from?" I ask.

"Absolutely," they say.

Then I pause for effect and say something like the following: "It sounds to me like you consider money to be more important than people, because you just told me you will do whatever it takes to connect every penny to a specific donor, but you don't spend the same kind of effort to track who's been coming lately—unless they've been putting money in the till."

I don't have to say much more.

They get the point.

It's hard to argue with.

CHAPTER 16

WHAT WE ARE IS WHAT WE'LL GET

In one sense, every leader leads by example, even those who don't realize it.

That's because at the end of the day, every follower is a boss watcher. They take their cues from what we do, not what we say. It doesn't matter if they're a volunteer, a member of a congregation, a part of a small group, or one of our kids.

As a former youth pastor, I learned this the hard way. I had the privilege of leading two youth ministries that appeared on the surface to be very successful. They were dynamic, filled with lots of kids, and life changing. At the time, I thought we were making a huge long-term impact for the kingdom.

But ten years later I realized the impact of my ministry was a lot less than I had thought. The majority of the kids who had been in my youth groups had grown up to become far more like their parents than the students they were in high school or college. They adopted the values, standards, and priorities of their parents.

Fortunately there were many cases where the biblical values, standards, and priorities I'd taught them as high schoolers and collegians aligned with what was modeled in their homes. There were also some outliers who permanently broke free of the family mold. But in most cases, it was the gravitational pull of their parents' example that won the day.

While I was thrilled that a large number continued to walk with God, I came to realize my role was a lot smaller than I'd thought. My example and teaching nudged them along the way. But it was the example set by the authority figures and leaders they spent the majority of their time with that had the most influence upon the kind of men and women they would become.

I shouldn't have been surprised.

JESUS SAID IT WOULD BE THIS WAY

Jesus said, "Everyone who is fully trained will be like their teacher" (Luke 6:40).

Notice what he didn't say. He didn't say that a fully trained disciple will become like what his teacher *teaches*. He said a fully trained disciple will become *like his teacher*.

One of the most important lessons every leader needs to learn is summed up in the old saying, "What you are is what you'll get." It's not what we say. It's not what we teach. It's who we are that matters most. The majority of people we lead will be far more impacted by our character and behavior than by the content of our curriculum.

One of the reasons Jesus so harshly condemned the

Pharisees was the toxic and contagious nature of their character. Many of the things they taught were actually spot on. At one point, Jesus even told his disciples to do what they said to do—but not what they did.[1] A few extra rules never killed anybody, but a harsh, judgmental, arrogant, and merciless character is a deadly spiritual cancer that spreads quickly.

SMALL THINGS MATTER

The key question every leader has to ask isn't, am I leading by example?

It's, what kind of example am I setting?

Most of us evaluate the example we're setting by the general pattern of our lives. We look at the big picture. But those who are watching us daily don't pay attention to the big picture as much as the exceptions. We tend to judge ourselves by our best moments. They tend to judge us by our worst moments.

If you're generally a laid-back, easygoing, let-it-slide leader, you'll probably see yourself as not easily angered. You'll think you're setting a stellar example of patience, turning the other cheek, bearing with others, and not taking offense. But all it takes is one road-rage incident while I'm in your car, and I'll never forget it.

It's the same with issues of honesty and integrity.

Small things matter.

For instance, we expect smart people to occasionally do dumb things. But we expect honest people to *always* be honest. One lie and the honest label is gone for good. That's why half-truths, disingenuous public praise, and euphemisms used to obscure uncomfortable facts have a far more negative impact than most of us realize. They erode trust, create cynicism, and model deceit in ways most of us miss.

THERE ARE NO SECRETS

As spiritual leaders we also need to understand that there are no secrets. If every follower is a boss watcher, a corollary is that they're well aware of lots of things we don't think they can see. The things we think no one knows about are often widely known and discussed in hushed tones when we're not around. And the things we think we've hidden well inevitably come to light when we least expect it.

Whether it's our congregation, staff members, volunteers, a coworker, or our own children, they see and know far more than we realize.

I first learned this principle when our church was small and I was able to do some counseling. Whenever I met with a struggling couple, I would ask them to tell me about their families of origin. Without fail, they would tell me lots of things their parents had no idea they knew about. This was true even in households where the parents worked hard to hide stuff. Whether it was a porn stash, a secret habit, debt collectors, closed-door arguments, infidelity, or any other carefully concealed secret or vice, the kids always knew.

They just never let on they knew. And more often than not, the things their parents thought they had hidden well ended up being a major contributor to the mess their kids were in years later.

Even our best-kept secrets seldom remain secrets for long. People talk.

The old axiom that three people can keep a secret as long as two of them are dead is true. Eventually, almost everything will come to light. Which is one reason I try to live my life by the newspaper rule: if I can't live with something being on the front page of the local newspaper, I just don't do it.

THE UNSEEN REALM

Even in those rare cases where the disparity between a leader's public and private life remains undisclosed, the example we set still has a powerful impact in the unseen realm. As we've already seen, secret sins have public consequences.

While it's difficult to chronicle and systematize exactly how the unseen realm works (after all, it is unseen), the reality of its impact is hard to dispute from a biblical perspective. Consider again the sin of Achan. He wasn't in any sort of leadership position. Yet his well-concealed thievery cost the Israelites dearly. Imagine how much greater the impact of a leader's secret sin can be. In some cases it can last for generations.

GENERATIONAL SIN

I've long been fascinated by the biblical concept of generational sins. It's the idea that even the unobserved actions of those in authority have a profound impact on those who are under their authority, and the impact can last for generations.[2]

Now that doesn't mean we can blame our sins and failings on Grandpa. Outside of the impact of Adam's sin, none of us is stuck because of what someone else did. We can't blame our rebellion on others. Ezekiel blew up any such fatalistic notions when he wrote:

> The word of the LORD came to me: "What do you people mean by quoting this proverb about the land of Israel:
>
> "'The parents eat sour grapes,
>   and the children's teeth are set on edge'?
>
> "As surely as I live, declares the Sovereign LORD, you will no longer quote this proverb in Israel. For everyone belongs to me, the parent as well as the child—both alike belong to me. The one who sins is the one who will die. . . .
>   "The child will not share the guilt of the parent, nor will the parent share the guilt of the child. The righteousness of the righteous will be credited to them, and the wickedness of the wicked will be charged against them." (Ezek. 18:1–4, 20)

But at the same time, there is a clear biblical pattern of unsavory behavior being passed on from one generation to the next. The actions of a father or spiritual leader often have an impact long after they've left the scene.

Perhaps the classic example of an unobserved generational sin being passed on to the next generation is the pattern of deception that Abraham passed on from one generation to the next.

It all started during a famine. Abraham went down to Egypt because there was food there. But since Sarah, his wife, was beautiful, he told her to tell everyone she was his sister so that no one would kill him to take her.

Now Sarah actually was his half-sister. So technically he wasn't asking her to lie. But the clear intent was deception. It was a *half-truth* told to *strangers* so things would go well for him. For a while, things got dicey, but in the end, everything worked out well, so he did it again years later when he temporarily moved to a place called Gerar.[3]

Many years later, Abraham's son Isaac faced a similar famine. He moved his family to Gerar to wait it out. When the men of Gerar asked him about his wife, he said, "She is my sister," because, like his father before him, he was afraid they might kill him to take her.

Now here's what's fascinating about his lie. He was not even born when Abraham instructed Sarah to lie. So it was not something Isaac saw and copied. It was a propensity to bend the truth under pressure that Abraham passed on to him in the unseen realm. But this time the lie was worse. It was not a half-truth. It was a *total lie*.

Many decades later, when Isaac was old and infirm, he decided it was time to pass on his blessing and inheritance to his oldest son, Esau. But his wife, knowing that God had prophesied the older would serve the younger, put together an elaborate ruse to trick Isaac into blessing Jacob, the youngest son.

Because Isaac was ailing and nearly blind, they were able to pull it off.

But at one point Isaac grew suspicious; he asked Jacob, "Are you really my son, Esau?"

"I am," Jacob told him.

So Isaac went ahead and gave him the sacred blessing and inheritance.

Abraham's pattern of deception had now reached the third generation. But this time it wasn't a *half-truth* told to a *stranger*. It wasn't a *total fabrication* told to a *stranger*. It was a *bold-faced lie* told to a *father* in order to *steal a brother's inheritance*.[4]

But that's not the end of story. It gets even worse. Many years later, ten of Jacob's twelve sons conspire to get rid of their younger (spoiled brat) brother, Joseph. They were tired of his boasting and their dad's blatant favoritism, so they sold him to a slave caravan and then told their father a wild animal had killed their brother.

Abraham's deceptive example had now reached full bloom. Ten of his great-grandsons had conspired to tell a *cruel and devastating lie* to their *father* to cover up a *heinous sin*.[5]

That's why leading by example is not optional. It's what we do, whether we realize it or not. The only question is, what kind of example are we setting? Because eventually the student will become the teacher. And whatever we are is what we'll get.

It's an irrefutable law of leadership.

SECTION 5
TAKE THE LONG VIEW

*When the Chief Shepherd appears, you will receive
the crown of glory that will never fade away.*

—1 Peter 5:4

CHAPTER 17

PATIENCE

For those of us who take on the mantle of spiritual leadership, patience isn't a virtue.

It's a necessity.

God's work moves along at his pace, not ours, and it's almost always at a lot slower pace than we'd prefer. Our impatience never spurs things along. It just throws sand in the gears. When Rebekah tried to help God out by making sure Jacob received the blessing and inheritance on her timetable, the result wasn't what she wanted. Her family was fractured, she never saw her favorite son again, and Jacob was forced to spend a huge chunk of his life on the run.

It was the same for Moses. His impatience cost him forty years in the wilderness.

As leaders, our greatest frustrations with God's timetable are most often found in three areas: (1) the spiritual growth of the *people* we serve, (2) the *fruit* that God produces, and (3) the *rewards* he promises. Let's take a look at each one to see the importance of maintaining a long-term perspective.

THE PEOPLE WE SERVE

Discipleship is always a long-term endeavor. Great starts are no guarantee of a happy ending, and horrific starts are sometimes the precursor to an incredible finish. We never know what we have until the last page is turned. It's a lot like parenting. We don't know what we've got until our kids hit thirty. Too many parents celebrate or panic too early. Most of us ended up a bit different than we were in seventh grade, our senior year in high school, or even college.

The typical spiritual journey is full of twists and turns. Who would have guessed that a power-hungry, hotheaded disciple named John would one day pen epistles as the Apostle of Love? Or that Saul, the enraged Jesus hater, would die as Paul the martyr?

It's always a mistake to either write off or lionize someone too quickly. But it's also always a great temptation. After a few weeks, few months, or even a few years we tend to mentally take a snapshot of people and then freeze-frame it as if that's where they'll be forever.

But that's not how discipleship works. The journey's never over until it's over. Consider the odd path of Joseph of Arimathea, one of my favorite examples of why we need to take the long view with the people we lead.

For all intents and purposes he was a spiritual loser. At least that's what most of us would have surmised. He fancied himself as a secret disciple. He was also a prominent member of the Sanhedrin, the seventy-one Jewish political and religious leaders who condemned Jesus as a blasphemer and turned him over to the Roman authorities to be crucified. While he didn't agree with or sign off on their decision, he also did nothing to stop it. He laid low in the weeds while the Messiah was railroaded on trumped-up charges because he feared the consequences of publicly identifying with Jesus. Remember, he was a prominent member of the group.[1]

Now let's be honest, most of us consider a secret disciple to be an oxymoron. We'd categorize Joseph as a disgrace, not a disciple. We'd not only write him off, we'd condemn him for his silence. After all, didn't Jesus say, "Whoever acknowledges me before others, I will also acknowledge before my Father in heaven. But whoever disowns me before others, I will disown before my Father in heaven" (Matt. 10:32–33)?

Except for one small problem.

The Bible calls Joseph a disciple.

Not once but twice.

And it doesn't say that he *became* a disciple when he came to his senses and boldly stepped forward to claim the body of Jesus. It says that he was a disciple (albeit a secret one) *before* any of that happened.[2]

Joseph represents what I call a "not yet ready" disciple. There are always more of them than we realize. It takes great patience and an incredibly long view of discipleship to keep from casting them aside, especially when they linger at the back of the line and never seem to make any progress.

Now I want to be clear. I am not excusing or justifying spiritual hesitancy. A secret disciple is a sucky disciple. No question. But it's not my job to prematurely determine the long-term fate of those whom God is not finished with yet. That's as ludicrous as firing a commissioned artist after a few strokes of the brush or even three-quarters of the way through a painting. It's not finished until it's framed.

Our job is to patiently steward the flock God has entrusted us with while he works out his ultimate plan and purpose for each of the lambs in it. He's the artist. We're the caretakers.

THE FRUIT GOD PRODUCES

Many of us are too quick to judge the fruit of God's blessing upon our ministries. There's an old saying that it takes fifteen years to become an overnight success. That might be rushing it a bit. The fact is that nothing of value happens overnight. Ministry is no exception. It doesn't matter if we're leading a small group of teenagers, planting a church, or leading an international ministry.

We often read the biblical accounts of answered prayer and miraculous fruit without an awareness of the underlying time frames. For instance, the events in the book of Acts took place over a thirty-year period. But since we can skim through the book in thirty minutes, we often expect God to reproduce the book of Acts in our lives and ministries in thirty days or fewer.

We want an avalanche. But God most often shows up as a glacier.

Avalanches are impressive, awe-inspiring, and powerful. They instantly alter the landscape, knocking down trees and burying everything in their path. Yet despite all the power and commotion they generate, their impact is relatively short term. If you come back a few years later, it's hard to tell where the avalanche took place. A decade later, only a trained eye would recognize the telltale signs. And a century later you'd have no way to examine its lasting legacy. Because it wouldn't have one.

Glaciers, on the other hand, are rather unimpressive. They don't appear to be doing much of anything. They just sit there. Or so it seems.

I spent one of the least exciting days of my life on an Alaskan cruise in Glacier Bay. While the scenery was amazing, the action was terminally boring. We waited for hours in the hopes of seeing a few large chunks of ice break off and fall into the sea. I'm told it's a spectacular sight. But we had no such luck. It was a day of watching ice melt.

It would have been much more exciting to watch an avalanche cascade down the mountain. But from a long-term perspective, the melting ice was doing something far more remarkable and spectacular than anything an avalanche could ever do. It wasn't knocking down trees. It was carving out a Yosemite.

The same thing happens in regard to God's work in the flocks we lead. He's often carving out a future Yosemite while we complain that nothing is happening. That's exactly what happened to me during my first five years at North Coast. I thought God was at work elsewhere. I was tempted to bail out. When I didn't see enough fruit on the vine, I was tempted to look elsewhere for better and more fertile soil.

I was an idiot. God was laying the groundwork for something far beyond anything I'd ever imagined.

An avalanche mind-set always makes it hard to stay the course. We'll continually think God isn't showing up, when in reality he's just not finished yet. We'll interpret every temporary setback as a disaster and panic at every extended dry spell.

THE REWARD GOD PROMISES

The third area where a spiritual leader needs to take an uncommonly long-range view is in regard to the rewards God promises. Those of us who shepherd well will receive a crown of glory that won't fade away. Guaranteed. It's God's promise. But it won't happen until the Chief Shepherd appears.[3]

That's not years down the road.

It's not at the end of our lives.

It's not even when we get to heaven.

It's when Jesus returns.

That's a lot longer than most of us have bargained for.

In our fast-paced, I-want-it-right-now, microwave world, that kind of delay is hard to get our minds around. For most of us a decade seems like a lifetime. Delayed gratification is hardly a modern-day cultural value. I know it's hard to fathom, but Peter and his contemporaries have already waited more than two thousand years for their ultimate reward. Who knows how much longer they'll have to wait?

That's not to say there aren't some amazing blessings and intrinsic rewards along the way. But from a biblical perspective, they are not the rewards we seek. They're merely samplings of what lies ahead.

While heaven is obviously awesome (it turns our greatest hardships into momentary light afflictions and our greatest earthly blessings into mere appetizers), the actual return of Jesus in glory will be better still. So much so that those who are already in heaven will shout for joy when the day arrives.[4]

Whenever we hit the wall and start to ask, "Is this worth it?" we need to step back and make sure we're asking the question from an eternal, not an earthly, perspective. Because in the short run, the answer will often be, "No, it's not worth it."

That's the lesson Asaph learned when he looked around and questioned the value of serving God when the wicked seemed to be prospering and the mockers mocked with impunity. Just when he was ready to throw in the towel, God revealed to him the destiny of the wicked and the reward of the righteous. It changed his perspective rather quickly.[5]

Long waits are par for the course when it comes to God's timing and his promised rewards. Abraham waited decades for his promised son, way too long from his and Sarah's perspective. His descendants waited four hundred years for their promised land. Those who longed for the Messiah to come had to wait centuries during a long and silent pause between the last Old Testament prophet and the birth of Jesus. And for the last two thousand years, every prophecy predicting the imminent return of Jesus has been proved wrong.

As Peter said in his second letter: "Do not forget this one thing, dear friends: With the Lord a day is like a thousand years, and a thousand years are like a day" (2 Peter 3:8).

Any time we fail to take the long view in regard to the people we serve, the fruit God produces, or the rewards he's promised, we set ourselves up for confusion and discouragement.

That's why patience isn't a virtue, it's a necessity when it comes to shepherding any of God's flock.

We might not always like God's timetable. In fact, we often won't. But last time I looked, he's God and we're not. So he gets to set the schedule and agenda. We get to carry it out.

CHAPTER 18

WAITING IN THE WINGS

It's never easy to wait.

Especially when you're young.

Perhaps that's why Peter wrote an addendum to those who were waiting in the wings in the hopes of one day climbing higher up the leadership ladder. Some of them may have been leaders already, but they were dreaming of the day when they would finally be in charge. Some may have simply been waiting for a chance to get into the game for the first time.

It doesn't matter, because whether their desire was to take on greater responsibility or they were simply looking for a chance to get into the game, the pathway to greater responsibility is exactly the same. Before we can lead well, we have to learn to wait well.

So after exhorting his fellow shepherds to keep a long-range perspective, he turned his attention to the younger leaders who were waiting their turn. He told them:

In the same way, you who are younger, submit yourselves
to your elders. All of you, clothe yourselves with humility
toward one another, because,

> "God opposes the proud
>> but shows favor to the humble."

Humble yourselves, therefore, under God's mighty
hand, that he may lift you up in due time. Cast all your
anxiety on him because he cares for you. (1 Peter 5:5–7)

In essence, he told them to do three things. The first is an
action step: submit to your current leaders. The second is an
attitude adjustment: clothe yourself with humility. And the
third is a step of faith: wait for God's perfect timing.

So let's step back and take a closer look at each of these.

SUBMIT TO YOUR LEADERS

At its core, the biblical concept of submission includes both obey-
ing the commands and complying with the desires of someone
else. It comes from a military term that generally involves submission to someone in authority over us, though the Bible also calls
for mutual submission between believers (and even spouses).[1]

In this case it's quite clear what Peter is referring to. He
wants younger leaders to comply with the commands and
wishes of those in spiritual authority over them. In modern-
day terms, he's simply asking them to serve them well. Be a
good lieutenant. Learn to follow well.

Now, obviously biblical submission isn't blind. Daniel didn't follow the king's edict to stop praying. His friends refused to bow down to Nebuchadnezzar's idol. And the apostles declined to stop preaching the gospel when they were commanded to do so.[2]

But it's important to note that while submitting to those in authority doesn't include doing that which is sinful, it does include doing things we don't like, agree with, or fully understand.

And it's here that a future leader's empathy for those he or she will lead is birthed. Give me leaders who have never learned to faithfully carry out orders they don't like, agree with, or understand, and I will show you leaders who have no understanding of what the people they lead are experiencing. I'll also almost certainly show you a leader who tends to be insensitive, demanding, and unreasonably harsh.

If we haven't learned to follow, we're not prepared to lead.

CLOTHE YOURSELF WITH HUMILITY

Humility is the second thing Peter says those who are waiting in the wings need to have. It's both an attitude and an action. It's an internal perspective that's fleshed out in our external behavior. The best modern-day phrase I can think of that combines both the internal and external reality of humility is showing respect.

Humility isn't taking on an artificially low opinion of ourselves. Jesus was humble, yet he claimed to be God in the flesh. That's hardly a golly-gee-whiz "I'm nothing" special brand of humility.[3] When he washed feet, took on the servant's role, and refused to seek his own revenge, he exemplified biblical humility. He treated others *as if* they were better or more important than he was.[4]

It's the same kind of humility Daniel showed toward Nebuchadnezzar. Even though he was a wicked king, Daniel submitted to his authority (as long as he wasn't commanded to do something sinful), and he showed tremendous respect in every encounter, which is why he continually advanced to greater and greater levels of responsibility.

It was the same with Joseph in Egypt. Like Daniel, he never seemed to complain about the injustice of his situation, the hardships, or the fact he was a more capable leader than everyone he served under. He just served them respectfully and well, and he kept getting promoted.

There is an old saying that if we want to be paid more for what we do, we need to do more than we are paid for. In the same way, if we want more responsibility, we need to do more than we are responsible for.

That's the path of promotion in a nutshell: respectfully serve those who are in authority over us. It's what happens when we combine biblical submission with genuine humility. We become promotable. We become prepared to lead.

EMBRACE GOD'S TIMING

The final ingredient we need in order to wait well in the wings is God's perfect timing. That sounds easy and passive. But it's not. It may be the hardest step of all.

God's will always has a what and a when. But unfortunately, many of us have been taught that once we know what God's will is, it's sinful to wait. We're supposed to respond immediately. So we don't even think to ask the "when" question.

That's always a huge mistake.

Let's look more closely at the mess Moses made of things when he stepped forward as Israel's deliverer forty years too soon. The Bible describes it in the following way:

When Moses was forty years old, he decided to visit his own people, the Israelites. He saw one of them being mistreated by an Egyptian, so he went to his defense and avenged him by killing the Egyptian. Moses thought that his own people would realize that God was using him to rescue them, but they did not. The next day Moses came upon two Israelites who were fighting. He tried to reconcile them by saying, "Men, you are brothers; why do you want to hurt each other?"

But the man who was mistreating the other pushed Moses aside and said, "Who made you ruler and judge over us? Are you thinking of killing me as you killed the Egyptian yesterday?" When Moses heard this, he fled to Midian, where he settled as a foreigner and had two sons.

After forty years had passed, an angel appeared to Moses in the flames of a burning bush in the desert near Mount Sinai. When he saw this, he was amazed at the sight. As he went over to get a closer look, he heard the Lord say: "I am the God of your fathers, the God of Abraham, Isaac and Jacob." Moses trembled with fear and did not dare to look.

Then the Lord said to him, "Take off your sandals, for the place where you are standing is holy ground. I have indeed seen the oppression of my people in Egypt. I have heard their groaning and have come down to set them free. Now come, I will send you back to Egypt." (Acts 7:23–34)

Now I've heard Bible teachers say that Moses needed to spend those forty years in the wilderness to prepare him for his great leadership task. But that's not what this passage says. It says that Moses jumped the gun. He knew *what* he was called to do (deliver Israel from their Egyptian slavery). But he didn't stop to ask *when*. As a result, he missed God's timing by forty years.

There's nothing in the text that says he needed to spend those forty years in the desert. The clear implication is the opposite. If he had waited for God's timing, he could have spent those forty years in the palace.

I don't know about you, but that strikes me as a far better option.

It's always a temptation for younger leaders to jump the gun just like Moses. Once we know what God has called and gifted us to do, we assume we're supposed to start today. And in our rush to get on with it, we end up in the wilderness, learning the lessons of submission and humility the hard way.

When a young leader learns to bloom where he or she is planted, it's generally not long until God lifts them up and transplants them into a new garden of greater influence and responsibility. But it always starts with serving well wherever we are right now. Because if we can't serve well here, we'll not lead well there.

EPILOGUE

FINAL THOUGHTS

Shepherding God's flock is one of life's greatest privileges. It's not for the faint of heart. It's not for the thin-skinned. It's not for the shortsighted. And it's certainly not for everybody.

As we've seen, leading like a shepherd is a choice. It's obedience, not leadership, that is required of us all. Daily obedience is the endgame for every disciple and the ultimate sign that we know and love God. Everything else is secondary.

But if you've taken on the mantle of this way of leading spiritually or you're aspiring to the role of an overseer, know that you are indeed pursuing a noble task. Just never forget that it won't make you a superior disciple or cause God to love you more or like you better. It's not a higher calling or a sign of greater commitment. It's just a different assignment.

In other words, stay humble. Don't think more highly of yourself than you ought. Keep your eyes dialed in on Jesus and how far you still have to go, rather than on your flock and how far they still have to go.

If you do, Peter's advice will serve you well. It's pure gold. It's simple. It's doable. It's within the reach of every spiritual leader no matter how small or large the flock may be. All we have to do is continually seek to

1. Think like a shepherd.
2. Serve with enthusiasm.
3. Lead by example.
4. Take the long view.

And finally, remember that at the end of the day, when we stand before Jesus, the health of our flocks will be far more important than the size of our flocks, and the way we shepherded his sheep will prove to be far more important than how many sheep we shepherded.

It's not the shepherd with the largest flock who receives a crown that won't fade away.

It's every shepherd who leads well.

rightnow MEDIA

FREE VIDEO CURRICULUM FOR

LEAD

LIKE A SHEPHERD
THE SECRET TO LEADING WELL

BECAUSE YOU HAVE PURCHASED
LEAD LIKE A SHEPHERD,
YOU ALSO HAVE FREE ACCESS TO THE
COMPANION VIDEO CURRICULUM - PERFECT
FOR GROUP STUDY OR PERSONAL DEVELOPMENT.

TO ACCESS THESE VIDEOS FOR 90 DAYS,
VISIT RightNowMedia.org/LeadLikeAShepherd
AND USE PROMO CODE: LLAS90

ACKNOWLEDGMENTS

I want to express my gratitude to Dave Travis, Greg Ligon, and Linda Stanley. You have helped me become a better leader and shepherd, and you have continually opened doors for me to teach and empower others with the lessons I've learned along the way.

I also owe a deep debt of gratitude to the elders, staff, and congregation at North Coast Church. Serving you has been one of the great privileges of my life. You're the best flock any pastor could hope for.

Erica Brandt, your careful eye and suggested corrections of my sometimes-goofy syntax has been invaluable. Thank you for your many years of faithful service.

Finally, I want to thank my amazing and beautiful wife, Nancy, a wise and candid sounding board, best friend, and soul mate all wrapped into one. I'm a lucky man.

NOTES

Chapter 1: Lead Like a Shepherd
1. See Matthew 28:18–20; 16:18.
2. See 1 Corinthians 3:10–15.
3. See 1 Peter 5:1–5.

Chapter 2: Am I Qualified?
1. See John 21:15–19. Some Greek scholars view the use of two different words for "love" in this passage to be insignificant, even synonymous. Others see the choice of words as not only significant, but as the key to understanding the passage. My own study and research into the debate leads me to believe that the choice of words is indeed significant and is the key to understanding the passage.
2. See Acts 4:13.
3. See 1 Timothy 3:1–13; Titus 1:5–9.
4. See Matthew 27:51; 1 Peter 2:9; and 1 Timothy 2:5.
5. See Hebrews 10:1–14 and 1 Timothy 2:5. The blood of bulls and goats could not permanently take away sins but only buy time, much like an interest-only payment forestalls foreclosure but never pays off a debt.

6. See 2 Corinthians 7:10.
7. See 1 Timothy 3:1–13 and Titus 1:5–9.
8. See Galatians 2:11–14.
9. See Acts 13:1–13; 15:36–41.

Chapter 3: No One Said It Would Be Easy

1. "Poll: American Trust in Clergy Members Hits All Time Low," CBS DC, December 16, 2013, http://washington.cbslocal.com /2013/12/16/poll-american-trust-in-clergy-members-hits-new-low/.
2. See 1 Timothy 3:2–7 and Titus 1:6.
3. Adam Taylor, "Why Mother Teresa Is Still No Saint to Many of Her Critics," *Washington Post*, September 1, 2016, https://www .washingtonpost.com/news/worldviews/wp/2015/02/25/why -to-many-critics-mother-teresa-is-still-no-saint/?utm_term =.985617cd5870.
4. See 1 Corinthians 5:9–13.
5. See Romans 12:2.

Chapter 4: The Original Peter Principles

1. NIMBY is an abbreviation of the phrase "not in my backyard," referring to opposition to a proposal for new development by nearby residents.
2. Laurence J. Peter and Raymond Hull, *The Peter Principle: Why Things Always Go Wrong* (New York: Morrow, 1969).

Chapter 5: It's All About the Sheep

1. See 1 Samuel 16:10–11.
2. See Ezekiel 34.
3. See Matthew 20:25–28.
4. See Acts 12:17; 14:4–7; 17:1–14; Matthew 10:14; Romans 1:10–13; 15:20–29.
5. See Acts 16:6–10.

Chapter 6: Willing to Be Misunderstood

1. See Numbers 13–14.
2. Andrew Ewers, "Effective Treatment to Control Lice," Sheep Connect South Australia, http://www.sheepconnectsa.com.au /technical-information/effective-treatment-to-control-lice.

Chapter 7: Adapting to Weakness

1. See John 8:1–11; Luke 18:9–14; Mark 9:17–27; and Matthew 11:19.

Chapter 9: Adapting to Fear

1. See Romans 12:2 and 2 Timothy 3:16–17.
2. For more on this model, see Larry W. Osborne, *Sticky Church* (Grand Rapids: Zondervan, 2008).
3. See Acts 8:1.

Chapter 10: Pursuing the Straggler

1. See Luke 10:1–18 and John 13:29.
2. See 2 Chronicles 26:1–23.
3. See Matthew 7:1–2; 18:21–35.
4. See John 20:24–29 and Luke 24:13–35.

Chapter 11: Flock Focused

1. See 1 Corinthians 5:1–13.
2. See Romans 5:12 and 1 Corinthians 15:22.
3. See Joshua 7:1–26.
4. See 1 Corinthians 5:1–13 and Titus 3:10.

Chapter 12: Privileged to Serve

1. See Mark 12:30–31 and Philippians 2:3–5.
2. See 2 Timothy 2:2.
3. See Romans 12:6–8.
4. See Matthew 26:36–46.

Chapter 13: The No Complaining Rule
1. See Luke 11:1–13; 18:1–8.

Chapter 14: Servant Leaders
1. See Matthew 15:1–14 and Mark 3:1–6.

Chapter 15: Shepherds and Cowboys
1. See Luke 11:1–13.
2. See 1 Peter 5:3.
3. See Matthew 23:3–4.
4. See Matthew 18:12–13.

Chapter 16: What We Are Is What We'll Get
1. See Matthew 23:3.
2. See Exodus 20:5; 34:7; Numbers 14:18; Deuteronomy 5:9.
3. See Genesis 12:10–20; 20:1–8.
4. See Genesis 27:1–46.
5. See Genesis 37:1–36.

Chapter 17: Patience
1. For a deeper dive into the spiritual journey of this complex disciple, see Larry Osborne, *Accidental Pharisees: Avoiding Pride, Exclusivity, and the Other Dangers of Overzealous Faith* (Grand Rapids: Zondervan, 2012).
2. See Matthew 27:57; Luke 23:50–51; and John 19:38.
3. See 1 Peter 5:4.
4. See 2 Corinthians 4:16–18 and Revelation 19:1.
5. See Psalm 73:1–28.

Chapter 18: Waiting in the Wings
1. See Ephesians 5:21–22.
2. See Daniel 6:6–10; 3:1–18; and Acts 5:27–42.
3. See John 5:18.
4. See Philippians 2:3–11 and John 13:1–17.

ABOUT THE AUTHOR

Dr. Larry Osborne is a senior pastor at North Coast Church and a mentor and coach to ministry and business leaders across the country.

His groundbreaking book *Sticky Church* ignited a nationwide movement of sermon-based small groups that gather weekly to discuss and apply the content of the previous weekend's sermon. This simple and organic small group model has enabled churches to exponentially increase their small group participation. At North Coast Church, participation exceeds 90 percent of weekend attendance.

Widely known for their innovative approach to leadership and ministry, Larry and North Coast Church also pioneered the concept of Video Venues, which laid the foundation and fueled the rapid growth of today's multisite churches.

Larry has a deep love for Scripture and a commitment to accurate and practical biblical teaching in a local church context. During his tenure as a teaching pastor at North Coast Church weekend attendance has grown from 128 to more than 12,000.

His books include *Thriving in Babylon, Accidental Pharisees, A Contrarian's Guide to Knowing God, 10 Dumb Things Smart Christians Believe, Mission Creep, The Unity Factor, Sticky Teams, Sticky Church,* and *Sticky Leaders.* There is no truth to the rumor that his next book will be titled *Sticky Fingers.*

Dr. Osborne holds both MDiv and DMin degrees from Talbot Theological Seminary. In addition to his work as a pastor, author, and leadership coach, he is also the founder and president of the North Coast Training Network.